FLAVOURS OF THE WEST COAST

A cookbook from the celebrated TV series

FLAVO

Our beautiful west coast—the Inside Passage.

URS
of the West Coast

Cedarwood Productions **with Chef Steve Walker-Duncan** and **guests**

TouchWood
Editions

TouchWood Editions
touchwoodeditions.com

LIBRARY AND ARCHIVES CANADA CATALOGUING IN PUBLICATION
Flavours of the west coast / Cedarwood Productions with Steve Walker-Duncan and guests.

Includes index.
Also issued in electronic formats.
ISBN 978-1-927129-24-1

1. Cooking, Canadian—British Columbia style. 2. Cooking—British Columbia.
3. Cookbooks I. Walker-Duncan, Steve II. Cedarwood Productions Inc

TX715.6.F52995 2012   641.59711   C2012-902163-6

Editor: Holland Gidney
Design: Pete Kohut
Cover photo: Karen Davies
Interior photos by Karen Davies and Lindsay Nielsen, unless otherwise indicated.

We gratefully acknowledge the financial support for our publishing activities
from the Government of Canada through the Canada Book Fund, Canada
Council for the Arts, and the province of British Columbia through the
British Columbia Arts Council and the Book Publishing Tax Credit.

This book was produced using FSC®-certified, acid-free paper,
processed chlorine free and printed with soya-based inks.

The information in this book is true and complete to the best of the authors' knowledge.
All recommendations are made without guarantee on the part of the author.
The authors disclaim any liability in connection with the use of this information.

1 2 3 4 5 16 15 14 13 12

PRINTED IN CHINA

This book is dedicated to our local food producers, whose drive to provide delicious, healthy, sustainable, and ethical produce makes British Columbia food some of the best in the world. Thank you.

One of the many stunning sunsets off the coast of Port Hardy.

Contents

The Cedarwood crew at work in the studio kitchen.

Foreword

Every four years, Canada enters a team in the International Culinary Olympics, which, like their sporting equivalent, is the most prestigious and demanding cooking competition in the world. Team Canada consistently places in the top six at this competition, even being crowned as world champions on one occasion. No mean feat considering that Canada is up against the traditional culinary giants of the world! What isn't as well known is the fact that for the majority of those years Team Canada was represented by chefs from British Columbia.

Here on the West Coast, we not only have a fabulous range of produce and natural food resources, but we also have some of the most talented and inspired chefs in the world. Treating the wonderful ingredients found here in the West with respect for their natural taste, and combining that respect with personal culinary inspiration and background influences, these chefs are creating truly outstanding dishes.

Many of the chefs in this book have represented Team Canada over the years. Some of them have long, successful careers behind them, with many honours and awards collected, while others are rising young stars, whom you will no doubt be hearing more from in the future. What all the contributing chefs share (apart from talent, obviously!) is a dedication to local food and sustainable food production. As the producer of the TV series *Flavours of the West Coast*, it has been my great privilege to work with these chefs and I am now thrilled to be able to share with you some of their signature dishes. And where a recipe is not identified by the name of one of our guest chefs, it is the creation of the show's host, the talented Chef Steve Walker-Duncan.

There is so much choice and quality available in British Columbia, and more and more producers and chefs are committing to supporting local ingredients and celebrating the fabulous food that BC offers. Not only is buying local better for our health and for our environment, but it also, quite simply, tastes better! So we invite you to delve into this book and to discover the creations of these inspirational chefs. You will find recipes for old favourites and also explore new ingredients and new recipes that will hopefully lead you to enjoy the finest flavours of the West Coast.

Wishing you much enjoyment in the process,

Karen Davies
Producer, *Flavours of the West Coast*

Introduction

The passion, determination, and dedication of all the people we have met while filming *Flavours of the West Coast* around our spectacular province has been nothing short of overwhelming. I am constantly amazed at the lengths to which these folks will go to in order to make amazing food and drink, as well as create markets, adapt to customer demands, and educate people about the benefits of healthy food.

After nearly 30 years in the food service industry, I was thrilled to be given the opportunity to explore and discover all of the bounty in our little piece of heaven here on the West Coast as I ate my way throughout the province. Without a doubt, we live in one of the finest places on earth to eat local, ethically sound, and delicious foods year-round.

I would like to wholeheartedly thank all of the chefs and cooks who generously gave their time to be a part of the show, and who remained patient while having a film crew descend upon their kitchens while they maintained production for their guests. The producers of all the wonderful fresh products we have access to must be given proper recognition as well, because without them our jobs as cooks would be much harder and less satisfying. As cooks, we really don't warrant all the credit for our creations because with great raw ingredients at our fingertips, we simply have to present them well and let the food speak for itself.

Without the love and support of our families, many of our endeavours would never happen. I have been blessed with a strong community of family and friends, which mirrors the strong food community that we've witnessed throughout our travels with *Flavours of the West Coast*. Building community has been a major strength for all of the people and places we have visited. Only with strong local relationships can we sustain environmental, economic, and personal stability and growth. Please continue to enjoy good food, support sustainable regional producers, and buy local.

Happy cooking!

Steve Walker-Duncan, CCC
Host, *Flavours of the West Coast*

CBC's Tony Parsons stars as Rookie Chef in the studio kitchen.

Nothing is better than home-grown herbs.

Basic Sauces

What do chefs mean when they casually use words such as roux or béchamel? These simple sauces and dressings are the foundation of so many recipes. Chefs know these basics by heart and once you do, too, you will be able to expand your repertoire to create your own versions of sauces and dressings that will soon become family favourites. Many of the sauces and dressings in this chapter also appear among the ingredients of other recipes.

and Dressings

Basic Vinaigrette

Makes 2 cups (500 mL)

½ cup (125 mL) freshly squeezed lemon juice (1 large lemon)

2 tsp (10 mL) Dijon mustard

2 Tbsp (30 mL) finely chopped parsley (optional)

2 tsp (10 mL) finely chopped chives (optional)

1 tsp (5 mL) dried chilies (optional)

salt and pepper, to taste

1½ cups (375 mL) canola or sunflower oil

If you have a strong arm for whisking, you can make this basic dressing. For a bolder flavour, use ½ cup (125 mL) olive oil and 1 cup (250 mL) neuturally flavoured oil, such as vegetable, sunflower, or canola oil.

1. In a medium bowl, combine all ingredients except for oil and mix thoroughly.
2. Slowly add oil while whisking vigorously.
3. If the dressing is not used immediately, then re-whisk before using.

Chef's Tip: To extract the maximum amount of juice, heat the lemon in a microwave for 30 seconds on full power, then roll with the palm of your hand on a flat surface a couple of times before squeezing.

Chef's Tip: Store the vinaigrette in a closed jar or bottle in the fridge for up to 2 weeks and shake well before using.

Creamy Cocktail Sauce

Makes 1 cup (250 mL)

There's only one thing to be said for this sauce: it's dippin' good! Use for dipping your favourite seafood.

1. In a medium bowl, mix together all ingredients.

Chef's Tip: Store in a closed jar or bottle in the fridge for up to 1 week.

¾ cup (185 mL) mayonnaise (p. 8)

3 Tbsp (45 mL) tomato ketchup

1 Tbsp (15 mL) fresh horseradish, grated (or 2 Tbsp/30 mL prepared horseradish sauce)

lemon juice, to taste

salt and pepper, to taste

Fishing for trout on Chapman Lake.

Mayonnaise

Makes 5 cups (1.25 L)

3 egg yolks

1 whole egg

1 tsp (5 mL) salt

1 tsp (5 mL) mustard powder

4½ cups (1.125 L) sunflower oil

2 tsp (10 mL) lemon juice

2 tsp (10 mL) white vinegar

1 tsp (5 mL) Worcestershire sauce

1 tsp (5 mL) cayenne pepper

salt and pepper, to taste

What doesn't taste better with mayonnaise smeared all over it? Make your own and you can change the flavour slightly, adding more cayenne or Worcestershire sauce if that's how you like it.

1. In a stainless steel mixing bowl, whisk egg yolks, whole egg, salt, and mustard powder until light and fluffy.

2. Whisking constantly, gradually add half of the sunflower oil in a slow, steady stream. The mixture should look uniform and homogeneous at all times. If it doesn't appear that way, stop adding oil and continue whisking until it's smooth and creamy looking.

3. Add lemon juice and vinegar, then add remaining oil. (The oil may be added more quickly at this point.)

4. Finish by stirring in remaining ingredients. Refrigerate immediately.

Chef's Tip: An electric mixer may be used instead of the whisk.

Chef's Tip: Store the mayonnaise in a closed jar in the fridge for up to 2 weeks.

Béchamel Sauce

Makes 4 cups (1 L)

This creamy white sauce can be used as a base for almost anything. If you want to keep the calories down, replace the whipping cream with milk.

1. In a heavy-bottomed pot, melt butter, then add onion and bay leaf. Sauté over moderate heat for 3–4 minutes, until onion is translucent but not browned.
2. Add flour and blend well, then cook for 2–3 minutes to make a white roux. (Watch for the edges touching the bottom of the pot to turn from a buttery yellow to a much paler, almost white colour.)
3. Add milk one-third at a time, stirring constantly. After each addition, be sure milk is fully incorporated before adding more.
4. Once all milk is in the pot, add whipping cream and bring back to a simmer.
5. Season with salt and pepper, then strain. For best results, use immediately.

Chef's Tip: To scald milk, warm milk in a pan over a moderate heat until just before it comes to a boil; do not allow to boil.

¼ cup (60 mL) butter
3 Tbsp (45 mL) diced onion
1 small bay leaf
¼ cup (60 mL) flour
4 cups (1 L) milk, scalded (see Chef's Tip)
½ cup (125 mL) whipping cream
salt and white pepper, to taste

Menu at Limbert Mountain Farms, Agassiz.

Mornay Sauce

Makes 4 cups (1 L)

4 cups (1 L) béchamel sauce (p. 9)

¼ cup (60 mL) grated fresh Parmesan cheese

2 Tbsp (30 mL) cold butter, broken into small pieces

1. Reheat béchamel sauce in a pot over low heat, then add Parmesan and butter.
2. Stir thoroughly until cheese is melted.

Alfredo Sauce

Makes 2 cups (500 mL)

2 Tbsp (30 mL) butter

1 Tbsp (15 mL) puréed garlic

1 cup (250 mL) béchamel sauce (p. 9)

1 cup (250 mL) whipping cream

¼ cup (60 mL) grated fresh Parmesan cheese

1 Tbsp (15 mL) finely chopped fresh parsley

Creamy, simple, and delicious, alfredo is a staple sauce that everyone should know how to make from scratch.

1. Heat a heavy saucepan over moderate heat, then add butter and garlic. Cook until garlic just begins to colour.
2. Add béchamel sauce and whipping cream, bring to a simmer, and then add Parmesan. Cook for 3–4 minutes, or until cheese is fully melted.
3. Stir in parsley and serve immediately over fresh linguini or your favourite pasta.

Tartar Sauce

Makes 2 cups (500 mL)

A dip and a jump is how long it will take you to make this delicious sauce. Serve with fish and chips.

1. Combine all ingredients and mix well.

Chef's Tip: Store in a closed jar in the fridge for up to 2 weeks.

2 cups (500 mL) mayonnaise (p. 8)
¼ cup (60 mL) finely chopped pickles
2 Tbsp (30 mL) finely chopped fresh parsley
3 Tbsp (45 mL) freshly squeezed lemon juice (about half a lemon)
1 Tbsp (15 mL) chopped capers
1 tsp (5 mL) mustard
salt and pepper, to taste

Certified Chef de Cuisine **Steve Walker-Duncan** has spent 31 years in the culinary industry, working in Canada, England, Holland, Spain, and Gibraltar. Guests for whom he has prepared his delicious creations include members of the royal family and many music and film celebrities. A former president and vice-president of the Victoria branch of the Canadian Culinary Federation, Walker-Duncan is passionate about his community and locally sourced products. Currently, he is giving to back to his craft as a certified cook assessor for the industry training authority of BC and working as a culinary instructor at Camosun College. In his "spare" time, Walker-Duncan enjoys hosting *Flavours of the West Coast*, shown every week on CHEK TV. He lives in Victoria, British Columbia.

Hollandaise Sauce

Makes 2 cups (500 mL)

5 egg yolks

2 Tbsp (30 mL) hollandaise reduction (p. 13)

1 lb (500 g) clarified butter, warm (see Chef's Tip)

salt and pepper, to taste

Tabasco sauce, to taste

This recipe is definitely a lot more work than just buying the packaged product, but the end result is worth the effort. Hollandaise is best known as being served on eggs Benedict, but it can also be served on top of veggies, such as asparagus.

1. Place egg yolks, hollandaise reduction, and 2 tablespoons (30 mL) water in a stainless steel bowl. Position bowl over the top of a pot of boiling water, then whisk steadily until mixture becomes slightly thick and fluffy.

2. Remove the bowl from the pot of water and continue beating for a few seconds.

3. While beating egg yolk mixture constantly, slowly add clarified butter.

4. Season with salt, pepper, and Tabasco. If the sauce is too thick, taste, then add a few drops of water or more reduction to thin it.

5. Scrape the sides of the bowl with a rubber scraper, cover the sauce, and keep warm until ready to serve. Surplus sauce may be placed in a covered container and refrigerated for future use for up to 1 week.

Chef's Tip: To clarify butter, melt butter over low heat, then pour off butter fat that rises to the top.

Hollandaise Reduction

Makes ¼ cup (60 mL)

1. In a small saucepan, combine all ingredients with ⅓ cup (80 mL) water and place over medium heat. Reduce by half.
2. Strain and reserve extra reduction for later use.

¼ cup (60 mL) lemon juice
1 Tbsp (15 mL) white wine vinegar
2 Tbsp (30 mL) chopped onion
10 white peppercorns, cracked
1 bay leaf

Cormorants and gulls in Hecate Strait.

1000 Island Dressing

Makes 2 cups (500 mL)

1½ cups (375 mL) mayonnaise (p. 8)

¼ cup (60 mL) tomato ketchup

1 Tbsp (15 mL) chopped black olives

1 Tbsp (15 mL) chopped dill pickles

1 Tbsp (15 mL) chopped green olives

1 Tbsp (15 mL) roughly chopped capers

1 tsp (5 mL) lemon juice

1 tsp (5 mL) finely chopped fresh parsley

1 hardboiled egg, peeled and diced small

1 tsp (5 mL) minced garlic

1 tsp (5 mL) Tabasco sauce

salt and pepper, to taste

As a child, salad wasn't quite the same unless it was submerged in this delicious, creamy dressing. As an adult . . . well, not much has changed. This dressing is easy to make and it will last for weeks in the fridge.

1. Combine all ingredients and mix well.

Chef's Tip: If using a food processor, quickly pulse whole olives, pickles, capers, egg, and parsley before adding all other ingredients and blending very briefly.

Chef's Tip: Store the dressing in a closed jar in the fridge for up to 2 weeks.

Sunset at sea.

Rosemary and Garlic Infused Vinegar

Makes 3 cups (750 mL)

This gorgeous vinegar can be made for your own use, or given as a gift. To make it look gift-worthy, seal the wine bottle with a cork and dip the end of the bottle into melted paraffin wax before tying on a label or ribbon.

4 large cloves garlic

3 cups (750 mL) white wine vinegar

½ tsp (2 mL) coarse sea salt

2 large sprigs fresh rosemary

coarse sea salt and whole black peppercorns, to taste

1. Peel garlic cloves, then bruise them by pressing down firmly with the side of a broad knife.

2. Add vinegar, garlic, and salt to a stainless steel saucepan. Bring to a boil for 2 minutes.

3. Allow to cool completely.

4. Meanwhile, wash rosemary sprigs well and place into a clear 26-ounce (750 mL) wine bottle with salt and peppercorns.

5. Using a funnel, strain the cooled vinegar into the wine bottle and seal it.

Chef's Tip: Other herbs, such as tarragon, thyme, or dill, may be used in place of the rosemary. Have fun experimenting!

Basil Pesto

Makes ½ cup (125 mL)

1 cup (250 mL) fresh basil leaves

⅓ cup plus 1 Tbsp (100 mL) olive oil

1.75 oz (50 g) pine nuts

2 cloves garlic, chopped fine

salt, to taste

¼ cup (60 mL) finely grated Parmesan cheese

1 Tbsp (15 mL) finely grated Romano cheese

2 Tbsp (30 mL) soft butter

Ah pesto! A teaspoon of this wonderful mix instantly takes you to summertime, even in the depths of winter!

1. Soak and wash basil in cold water. Dry with paper towel.
2. Add basil, olive oil, pine nuts, garlic, and salt to a food processor and process to a creamy consistency.
3. Transfer to a bowl and mix in cheeses and butter by hand.

Chef's Tip: When using pesto over pasta, dilute if needed with 1 or 2 tablespoons (15–30 mL) of the hot water in which the pasta was cooked.

The old cannery at Port Edwards.

Roux

Makes 1 cup (250 mL)

Roux is one of the most basic thickeners in cooking. It can be used to thicken almost any liquid.

½ cup (125 mL) butter, margarine, meat fat, or vegetable oil
½ cup (125 mL) flour

1. In a heavy saucepan, heat the fat, then incorporate the flour until a smooth paste forms.

2. Cook over a moderate heat until desired colour is achieved:
   - White roux will "pale" as the starches cook, meaning the flour will lighten up initially before starting to brown.
   - Blonde roux is the next stage after white roux, when the colour becomes a light tan.
   - Brown roux is when the colour becomes a deeper brown, but not too dark or it will become bitter. (A good indicator is to compare the colour of a used wooden spoon or a wooden cutting board against the roux.)

3. When adding liquid to the roux, allow the roux to cool slightly, and warm (but not boil) the liquid before adding it.

4. Add liquid one-third at a time, stirring constantly and vigorously (yet carefully as the first third will create quite a stiff dough-like mixture), allowing it to come to a boil before adding the next third of liquid.

5. Following each addition of liquid, it is imperative to stir the roux until it has a very smooth consistency before adding the next third of liquid to work out all of the lumps.

Chef's Tip: Roux can be made in a variety of "colours." White roux is used for light, milk-based sauces or soups; blonde roux is used for lightly coloured sauces utilizing stocks or coloured liquids; and brown roux is for richer, darker sauces and gravies, providing a more robust deeper colour. The thickening power a roux provides is reduced the more the flour is browned, so you need to add more brown roux to achieve the same consistency as with a white roux.

Crème Anglaise

Makes 2½ cups (650 mL)

2 cups (500 mL) milk

½ cup plus 3 Tbsp (170 mL) sugar, divided

6 large egg yolks

1 tsp (5 mL) vanilla extract

One of those patisserie staples that everyone loves!

1. Pour milk into a heavy saucepan and sprinkle 3 Tbsp (45 mL) of the sugar over the top but do not stir it in. Bring to a boil.

2. In a stainless steel bowl, beat egg yolks and remaining sugar with vanilla.

3. While stirring slowly, pour in the hot milk.

4. Pour mixture back into the saucepan and stir continuously over low heat with a wooden spoon just until it begins to thicken. (Do not overheat or the eggs will overcook and look like scrambled eggs!)

5. Remove from heat and pour back into the bowl to prevent further cooking.

6. Allow to cool and use for your favourite dessert.

Chef's Tip: The simplest way to use crème anglaise is to half-fill sweet pastry cups and top with your favourite fresh fruit. Simple, delicious, and always impresses guests!

Lemon Curd

Makes 2 cups (500 mL)

A traditional spread that won't give you a sour face, this lemony delight can be spread on a scone with afternoon tea, or used as a pastry filling.

1. In a heavy saucepan, whisk together sugar, eggs, lemon juice and zest, and a pinch of salt.

2. Add butter all at once and cook over moderately low heat, whisking constantly until curd is thick enough to hold whisk marks and the first bubbles appear on its surface.

3. Immediately pour through a fine sieve into a bowl, then rub the warm surface of the curd with a small piece of cold butter. The butter will melt as you rub it.

4. Refrigerate in a closed jar or bottle until required.

Chef's Tip: Before zesting, wash lemons under very hot water to remove the wax coating.

¾ cup (185 mL) sugar

3 large eggs

1 cup (250 mL) freshly squeezed lemon juice

1 Tbsp (15 mL) finely grated fresh lemon zest (see Chef's Tip)

pinch of salt

⅔ cup (160 mL) unsalted butter, cut into pieces

The Inside Passage.

Forest

Beautiful roadside flowers on the road to Barkerville and Wells.

Could there be anything more satisfying for a foodie than making a delicious meal with ingredients you picked and foraged yourself? The West Coast is blessed with an abundance of wild foods that are available year-round. In this section, you will find recipes that use ingredients native to British Columbia, from wild game to our wonderful BC berries and mushrooms, and some more unusual but traditional ingredients, such as nettles and sea asparagus. Enjoy foraging and collecting, but please remember to only take what you need and harvest in a way that doesn't damage the plants, so that there will be plenty for future generations.

and Field

Braised Rabbit with Blueberries and Wilted Mustard Greens

Makes 4–6 servings

1 rabbit, skinned and cut into large pieces (or substitute free-range chicken)

salt and pepper, to taste

3 Tbsp (45 mL) vegetable oil (see Chef's Tip)

1 large onion, thinly sliced

4 plump garlic cloves, whole

1 tsp (5 mL) thyme, fresh or dried

2 cups (500 mL) rich chicken stock

3 bay leaves

4 medium-sized red-skinned potatoes, halved

½ cup (125 mL) frozen peas

½ cup (125 mL) blueberries, fresh or frozen

1 large bunch mustard greens (or spinach), washed and drained

Chef's Tip: Feel free to substitute butter or chicken fat for the vegetable oil if you prefer the taste.

Talk about free-range! Rabbit is one of the ultimate wild game foods, and it tastes delicious too. Add the combination of sweet blueberries with the sharpness of mustard greens to create a flavour profile that will make your taste buds pop.

1. Heat a flameproof casserole dish or ovenproof pan over moderate heat.

2. Season rabbit pieces with salt and pepper.

3. Add oil to the pan and sear all the pieces of meat until golden brown on all sides. Remove from pan and put aside.

4. Add onions and garlic to the pan and cook until golden, then add thyme, one-quarter of the chicken stock, and bay leaves.

5. Return the rabbit to the pan and add the potatoes. Add more chicken stock until rabbit is halfway covered. Cover tightly with parchment paper and place in 325°F (160°C) oven for 30 minutes.

6. Remove rabbit pieces, then place pan with potatoes on the stove over high heat and reduce sauce by half.

7. Add peas and blueberries and cook for 1 minute.

8. Meanwhile, warm a frying pan over moderate heat and add mustard greens and a good pinch of salt and pepper. Stir gently until wilted, drain well, and place on a warm serving platter.

9. Lay rabbit pieces and potatoes over the greens and pour sauce over the top. Garnish with fresh blueberries.

Pan Seared Venison Loin with Blueberries, Shallots, and Red Wine

Lochlan Smyth, Sous Chef, Crest Hotel, Prince Rupert

Makes 4 servings

1 small handful fresh-picked thyme leaves

5 dried juniper berries

sea salt and freshly ground black pepper

2 Tbsp (30 mL) extra virgin olive oil, divided

1¾ lb (625 g) venison loin, trimmed

4–5 shallots, peeled and thinly sliced

1 garlic clove, peeled and finely sliced

6 oz (180 mL) red wine (see Chef's Tip)

1 cup (250 mL) fresh blueberries

2 Tbsp (30 mL) butter

On average, venison has 40% fewer calories than beef because wild animals exercise more and consume a more natural diet than domesticated animals, which creates a leaner meat. Venison also has a rich, strong flavour that is delicious with herbs and wine, like in this tasty dish.

1. Bash thyme and juniper berries with a mortar and pestle with a pinch of sea salt and a bit of pepper. (If you don't have one, chop berries with a knife but make sure you crush them a bit under a pot first or they'll fly all over the place!)

2. Loosen the mixture with a bit of olive oil. Pat dry venison with paper towels and rub thoroughly with spice mixture.

3. Sear venison in a hot pan over medium-high heat, making sure to turn it about once a minute. Searing will take roughly 6 minutes for medium rare to a maximum of 7–8 minutes for medium. Remove venison from the pan and cover with foil while you make the sauce.

4. Using the same pan, reduce the heat and add a glug of olive oil.

5. Add shallots and garlic and fry gently for about 3 minutes, until translucent. Turn the heat back up, add wine, and reduce by half.

6. Add blueberries and simmer gently for about 4 minutes, then remove pan from heat and add butter. Swirl pan gently until butter is melted and sauce has a velvety, opaque appearance. Season to taste with sea salt and pepper.

7. Slice venison however you like, then spoon sauce over the top. (It's just that easy!) Serve with a nice, light salad of organic greens, fresh berries, toasted nuts, soft goat cheese, and a fruity vinaigrette.

Chef's Tip: Use either a light, fruity Merlot or a robust Shiraz, depending on how rich you want the dish to be.

Chef's Tip: I don't recommend cooking venison to any more than medium (7–8 minutes) since it is a very lean meat that can dry out and become tough if it's cooked too much.

Lochlan Smyth's career started at a very early age as he grew up with a mother who made everything from scratch. She taught him the importance of making real food instead of just opening a package. Lochlan started off making his own lunches when he was home from school. The first dish he ever made on his own was mushrooms fried in a wok with olive oil, garlic, basil, and oregano. That was when he was eight years old and he's never looked back! Lochlan's true love is international food, the fresh, vibrant cuisine from different cultures around the world. The rule he lives by is to eat fresh and healthy and to choose BC products whenever possible. Lochlan wants to thank Jamie Oliver for the inspiration to cook professionally and for bailing him out by providing a recipe for something he'd never cooked before. His campaign to improve the food being served to kids in schools, both in his native England and in North America, is a wonderful and noble mission that deserves massive respect!

Cork's Blackberry Jalapeno Sauce

Cook Courtney Bryant, Powell River

Makes about 1 cup (250 mL)

4 cups (1 L) dry red wine

2½ cups (625 mL) fresh blackberries

4 Tbsp (60 mL) butter

2 whole jalapeno peppers,
seeds removed and minced

salt, to taste

3 Tbsp (45 mL) honey

This sauce to end all sauces combines two things most people love: spice and wine. Serve over local seared halibut or even a piece of sockeye—this sauce isn't picky about what it's paired with, as long as it's fish! When choosing blackberries, the sweeter and fresher, the better.

1. Reduce wine until syrupy and one-quarter its original volume.

2. Crush blackberries through a sieve, composting the seeds and setting aside the pulp and juice for later use.

3. In a saucepan, sauté minced jalapenos in butter over medium heat. When softened, add salt and reserved blackberry juice and pulp along with wine reduction. Allow mixture to bubble and continue to reduce for 5 more minutes.

4. Add honey and taste. Add more honey and/or salt if necessary.

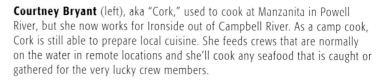

Courtney Bryant (left), aka "Cork," used to cook at Manzanita in Powell River, but she now works for Ironside out of Campbell River. As a camp cook, Cork is still able to prepare local cuisine. She feeds crews that are normally on the water in remote locations and she'll cook any seafood that is caught or gathered for the very lucky crew members.

After running the dining room at Manzanita for four years, **Amy Sharp** (right) is enjoying taking the show on the road. She loves vending gorgeous local shellfish and finfish, along with her famous pulled pork to smiling faces at street, prawn, and jazz festivals. Manzanita also provides catering to private islands, business meetings, weddings, and private parties.

Alpine flowers on Hudson Mountain, Smithers. The crew were all fighting to be the ones to go and get the pictures up there!

Creamed Nettles

Chef Jared Qwustenuxun Williams, Cowichan Valley

Makes 4–6 servings

Chef Jared says, "Eating stinging nettles raw is like eating a bumblebee. If you eat it head first, your mouth will be okay, but you'll probably still get stung on your hands." On the upside, nettles are safe and delicious when you cook them, plus they're free to pick and full of antioxidants.

1. Wash nettles under cold, running water, but beware, the nettles still sting!

2. Remove stems and set aside.

3. In a medium saucepan, place garlic, shallot, and butter. Warm pan over low heat just enough so the butter melts. Pour 1 cup (250 mL) of the whipping cream into the pan and season with salt and pepper.

4. Let cream reduce slightly to take in all the flavours of the shallot and the garlic.

5. Once about half-reduced, when the bubbles are getting big after 5–6 minutes, add nettles and pour in remaining cream, making sure nettles are thoroughly coated with cream. Let liquid reduce over low heat. (The nettles will release a liquid of their own, in turn thinning the cream.)

6. Bring nettles to a slow boil to get rid of their sting. The nettles will be completely wilted when they're finished: there will be no rigidity to the stems or the leaves; they almost become one with the cream and the cream will take on a bit of a green tinge.

7. Serve as a side dish, or serve around a base of mashed potatoes.

6 cups (1.5 L) nettles
(or mature spinach)

3 cloves garlic, chopped

1 shallot, chopped

1 Tbsp (15 mL) butter

1½ cups (375 mL) whipping
cream, divided

salt and pepper, to taste

Chef's Tip: Nettles retain their sting unless either submerged in water for 12 hours, boiled, or hung to dry for about a week.

Some interesting notes about nettles: There are many varieties of nettles and they grow all over the globe. Nettles are very popular in Nepalese and Northern Indian cuisines. They are high in nutrients, and it seems odd that in Canada they have been labelled as weeds when they're part of the spinach family. When you're picking nettles, look for young tender shoots because they have the most flavour.

Mushroom, Pepper, and Polenta Tartlets with Goat Cheese

Makes 6 servings

Polenta

1 large shallot, finely diced

2 cloves garlic, crushed

2 Tbsp (30 mL) olive oil

1 cup (250 mL) milk

½ cup (125 mL) cornmeal (polenta)

1 cup (250 mL) butter

1 Tbsp (15 mL) parsley, chiffonaded (see Chef's Tip)

1 Tbsp (15 mL) cilantro, chiffonaded (see Chef's Tip)

salt and pepper, to taste

clarified butter, for frying (see Chef's Tip, p. 12)

Traditionally, polenta was classified as peasant food and it is also known as "gruel." Embrace your inner peasant and try this dish: it's delicious, no matter what its history or caste. Try it as a party appetizer, or for lunch with a fresh green salad.

Polenta

1. In a heavy saucepan over medium heat, sweat shallot and garlic in olive oil without allowing them to colour, then add milk and 1 cup (250 mL) water. Bring to a boil.

2. While stirring constantly, sprinkle in cornmeal and continue stirring until polenta is fully cooked (the grains should be soft yet still have texture). This will take about 10–15 minutes.

3. Remove from heat and stir in butter until completely incorporated, then finish with parsley, cilantro, salt, and pepper.

4. While polenta is still hot, spread onto an oiled baking sheet, cover with buttered parchment paper (butter side down), and allow to cool completely.

5. Once cool, cut polenta into 6 large shapes, your choice of rounds, triangles, diamonds, or squares.

6. Heat a non-stick sauté pan with a little clarified butter and carefully brown both sides of polenta shapes before placing on a baking sheet. Set aside while you prepare the peppers and mushrooms.

Roasted Peppers and Portobello

1. Toss mushrooms and peppers with oil, garlic, rosemary, salt, and pepper, then roast in a 450°F (220°C) oven for 8–10 minutes, turning occasionally to ensure even cooking. If mushrooms look finished, remove them and set aside. Peppers should be well coloured and soft.

2. Place whole peppers into a container and cover with plastic wrap for 15 minutes and allow to cool. Once cool, remove their skins under running water. Remove seeds and membranes and cut each pepper into 6 thick strips.

3. To assemble, place polenta pieces on a baking sheet and place a mushroom, cup side up, on top. Top each mushroom with a goat cheese disc and two pepper strips, then bake for 8–10 minutes in a hot oven, until just warm. Finish with a tomato and fresh herb vinaigrette or another dressing of your choice, such as the recipe on page 6.

Chef's Tip: Leftover polenta trimmings can be diced up and used in salads.

Chef's Tip: To chiffonade, first wash parsley or cilantro with stems attached, then grip the stems like a bunch of flowers and, on a cutting board, roll the bunch of parsley into a nice, tight cigar shape. Slice through this roll of herb tops very thinly to create a chiffonade of herbs. Do not overchop.

Roasted Peppers and Portobello

6 medium portobello mushrooms
2 whole red peppers
3 Tbsp (45 mL) olive oil
2 cloves garlic, bruised
2 sprigs fresh rosemary
salt and pepper, to taste
1 tsp (5 mL) fresh thyme
(or ½ tsp/2 mL dried thyme)
6 1½ oz (40 g) discs of goat cheese

Creamy Mushroom Lentil Soup

Chef Michael Williams, Country Grocer

Makes 4–6 servings

2 Tbsp (30 mL) extra
virgin olive oil or butter

4 cups (1 L) white or brown button
mushrooms, quartered (about 12 large)

1 small leek, light-coloured
portion only, sliced thin

2 or 3 cloves garlic, minced

3 cups (750 mL) chicken
or vegetable broth

1 cup (250 mL) coconut milk

2 Tbsp (30 mL) fresh thyme leaves

4 cups (1 L) assorted
mushrooms (sliced)

sea salt and fresh ground
pepper, to taste

½ cup (125 mL) chopped
fresh Italian parsley

2 cups (500 mL) cooked red lentils

This delicious soup is totally dairy free because puréed mushrooms are used to thicken the base instead of other "thickeners." Chanterelle or morel mushrooms are perfect for the assorted mushrooms if you can find them; otherwise, portobellos, shiitakes, oysters, or a mix of all three works very well too. Allow 25 minutes preparation time and 25 minutes cooking time.

1. Preheat a large pot over medium-high heat.
2. Add oil and about half of the button mushrooms and sauté, stirring occasionally, until lightly browned. Add the remaining mushrooms and sauté until lightly browned. If you overload the pot, the mushrooms will never brown, hence cooking in batches.
3. Reduce heat to medium-low and add a touch more oil if necessary before adding the leek. Sauté for 3 or 4 minutes, stirring occasionally.
4. Add garlic and sauté for 2 minutes more, stirring frequently.
5. Add broth, coconut milk, and thyme, then simmer gently for 15 minutes. Remove soup base from heat for a couple of minutes to allow it to cool.
6. Using a food processor, blender, or immersion blender, purée the slightly cooled soup until very smooth. Return puréed contents to the pot, then season with salt and pepper to taste.

7. Preheat a large frying pan over medium-high. Add a little oil or butter and about half of the assorted mushrooms. Sauté until nicely browned and season with salt, pepper, and parsley. Set aside and repeat with remaining mushrooms.

8. Add sautéed assorted mushrooms and cooked lentils to the soup base, give it a taste for seasoning, then serve.

Chef's Tip: You can customize this recipe and make it your own by adding other sautéed veggies, such as celery, carrot, and onion, along with the assorted mushrooms.

Chef's Tip: Don't have coconut milk? Use cream or half-and-half if that is more accessible.

Chef Michael Williams creates great-tasting recipes that the whole family can prepare and enjoy together. Michael brings with him years of international experience in some of the finest kitchens and combines that with a solid understanding of nutrition and healthy cooking. He strives to create recipes using natural, local, and unprocessed foods found at any Country Grocer.

Barley and Mushroom Risotto

Chef Michael Williams, Country Grocer

Makes 3–4 servings

½ cup (125 mL) pot barley

1½ cups chicken stock, homemade
or storebought (see Chef's Tip)

2 Tbsp (30 mL) butter

2 cups (500 mL) assorted mushrooms,
divided (see Chef's Tip)

½ cup (125 mL) onion, diced very small

1 Tbsp (15 mL) minced garlic

2 Tbsp (30 mL) fresh thyme leaves

½ tsp (2 mL) sea salt (see Chef's Tip)

¼ tsp (1 mL) fresh
ground black pepper

½ cup (125 mL) coconut milk

½ cup (125 mL) grated
Parmesan cheese

¼ cup (60 mL) chopped parsley,
for garnishing (optional)

Chef's Tip: If you are using
storebought broth, make sure to use a
low-sodium version and omit the salt
from the recipe.

Chef's Tip: Oyster, shiitake, portobello,
or button mushrooms are all good
choices. If you can get your hands on
some wild mushrooms, use them. Morels
or chanterelles would both work well.

You can never replace a perfectly made risotto but, with health in mind, the white risotto rice has been replaced with whole-grain pot barley in this recipe. With minimal work, you end up with a delicious and creamy side dish worth making again and again.

1. Rinse barley and drain well.

2. In a medium pot, combine barley and stock. Bring to a boil and then immediately reduce heat to low and cover with a lid. Gently simmer for 25–30 minutes or until most of the liquid has been absorbed.

3. While barley is cooking, preheat a large frying pan over medium heat. Once pan is hot, add butter and half the mushrooms. Sauté, stirring occasionally.

4. Once mushrooms begin to brown, add remaining mushrooms and sauté, stirring occasionally until lightly browned.

5. Add onion and sauté for another few minutes, stirring occasionally.

6. Add garlic and thyme and sauté for about 1 minute more, stirring frequently.

7. Season with salt and pepper, then add coconut milk and remove from heat.

8. Once barley is cooked, combine with mushroom mixture and Parmesan. Stir to combine and garnish with parsley. Serve immediately.

Photo: Gregg Eligh

Mixed wild mushrooms.

Traditional Mushroom Risotto

Makes 4–6 servings

Serve this dish on its own or with medium-rare roasted pork tenderloin and some sautéed spinach. Portion out the risotto as soon as it's ready or the rice will continue to absorb liquid and dry out.

1. Warm a large saucepan over medium heat. Add oil, then sauté onion and garlic for 2 minutes until translucent; do not brown.

2. Add mushrooms and cook for 5–6 minutes, just until excess water has evaporated.

3. Add rice and stir thoroughly to coat every grain with oil.

4. Add one-third of the stock and simmer until almost all the liquid has evaporated. Repeat twice more. (The consistency can be adjusted by adding a little more stock.)

5. Stir in mascarpone and Parmesan until melted, then remove from heat and stir in butter. Season with salt and pepper.

6. Serve immediately.

Chef's Tip: Regular button mushrooms or rehydrated dried mushrooms can also be used. If using the latter, place mushrooms in a bowl and pour boiling water over the top and let soak for 20–30 minutes. Do not discard the liquid but add it to the stock.

3 Tbsp (45 mL) olive oil

¼ cup (60 mL) minced onion

2 cloves garlic, minced

1 cup (250 mL) assorted wild mushrooms, roughly chopped (see Chef's Tip)

1½ cups (325 mL) arborio rice

4 cups (1L) chicken or vegetable stock

¼ cup (60 mL) grated Parmesan

½ cup (125 mL) mascarpone cheese

3 Tbsp (45 mL) butter

salt and pepper, to taste

Warm Morel, Kale, and Burdock Salad

Chef Bill Jones, Cowichan Valley

Makes 4–6 servings

Burdock Garnish

4 cups (1 L) burdock root, scrubbed and julienned

1 carrot, peeled and julienned (optional)

1 Tbsp (15 mL) fresh ginger, shredded

3 Tbsp (45 mL) light soy sauce

2 tsp (10 mL) mirin

1 tsp (5 mL) sesame oil

1 tsp (5 mL) hot sauce (or chili paste)

This salad is a play on a traditional Japanese warm spinach salad called Gomae. Kale is one of the most nutritious vegetables in the garden and tastes amazing. Miner's lettuce is so called because it was the first edible green leaf to appear in the springtime, so it was vital for miners as a way to obtain their Vitamin C after a winter without. You can also use local burdock root to add a pleasing texture to the salad. This salad is great as a side dish or paired with pan-fried oysters or local spot prawns. It can also be prepared a day in advance.

Burdock Garnish

1. Simmer burdock, carrot (if using), and ginger in a saucepan over medium heat for 4–5 minutes. Add soy sauce, mirin, sesame oil, and hot sauce, then simmer for an additional 10 minutes. Set aside.

Deerholme Farm is a culinary destination in the heart of the Cowichan Valley that began attracting the attention of food lovers and international media the moment it opened.

Its owner, chef and food consultant **Bill Jones**, holds monthly themed dinners, cooking classes, and workshops in a renovated 1918 farmhouse on the property. Bill specializes in farm-to-table cooking and helps support a growing community of food producers and foragers throughout the Pacific Northwest. Bill is the author of nine cookbooks, winner of two world cookbook awards, and is known as a regional expert on wild foods, in particular mushrooms. *Gourmet*, *Food and Wine*, *Bon Appétit*, the *New York Times*, and other prominent media outlets have all profiled his work.

Salad

1. Add dried morels and kelp to a heatproof bowl. Cover with boiling water and let sit for 15 minutes.

2. Remove mushrooms and kelp and cut mushrooms into rings and kelp into thin strips. Prepare kale by stripping the leaves from the stems and chopping the leaves coarsely.

3. Add grapeseed oil, garlic, miso, and mirin to a non-stick skillet over medium heat. Once bubbling, add morels, kelp, miner's lettuce, and shredded kale; stir to mix. Cook for 2–3 minutes, or until kale wilts. Add vinegar, sesame oil, toasted sesame seeds, and pickled ginger. Toss to coat and warm through.

4. Transfer to a serving plate and top with burdock garnish and a sprinkling of additional sesame seeds. Serve warm or at room temperature for best flavours.

Salad

1 oz (30 g) dried morels
(or use 1 cup/250 mL fresh)

1 oz (30 g) dried bull kelp

1 lb (500 g) kale (or spinach)

1 cup (250 mL) miner's lettuce, or other local salad greens (optional)

1 Tbsp (15 mL) grapeseed oil

1 tsp (5 mL) fresh garlic, minced

1 Tbsp (15 mL) white miso paste

2 Tbsp (30 mL) mirin

1 Tbsp (15 mL) white wine vinegar

1 tsp (5 mL) sesame oil

1 Tbsp (15 mL) toasted sesame seeds

1 Tbsp (15 mL) pickled ginger

1 Tbsp (15 mL) burdock garnish

1 Tbsp (15 mL) sesame seeds

Chokecherry Soufflé

Chef Philippe Renaudat, Cutting Board Restaurant, Lytton

Makes 8 servings

2 cups (500 mL) chokecherries
(or your favourite berry)
2 cups (500 mL) sugar
1 lemon, juiced
4 eggs
2 egg yolks
¾ cup (185 mL) sugar
2 cups (500 mL) whipping cream
fresh wild berries
8 mint sprigs

This soufflé will tower above the rest–literally. Gorgeous pink in colour and light and fluffy on the palate, this dessert is original and delicious.

1. Place chokecherries, sugar, lemon juice, and ½ cup (125 mL) water into a saucepan over medium heat and stir, cooking for about 20 minutes.

2. Let mixture cool in the fridge.

3. Once cooled, mix using a hand blender, then strain out the juices over a bowl and set aside.

4. Place eggs, egg yolks, and sugar in a stainless steel bowl. Set bowl over a pan of simmering water, then whisk ingredients (or use an electric mixer) until the mixture becomes thick and creamy. Do not overcook! Allow to cool.

5. In a small bowl, whip cream until light but not too stiff. Incorporate chokecherry mixture and egg and sugar mixture. Fold in whipping cream gently.

6. Line 8 ramekins with parchment paper: tear off squares of paper and fold in half, placing inside ramekins so lining stands approximately 3 inches (8 cm) above the edge.

7. Pour soufflé mixture into these prepared dishes, filling each one to about 1 inch (2.5 cm) above the top of the ramekin.

8. Freeze for 3 hours. When ready to serve, remove paper from around the edges of the ramekins, and garnish soufflé with fresh wild berries and a sprig of mint.

Chef Philippe Renaudat was born in the village of Levroux, France, and his interest in cooking started in the kitchen with his mother. He attended cooking college in Châteauroux and then spent the next 40 years travelling and working at top restaurants around the world, including the Djibouti Palace Hotel in Somalia, the Auberge de Dior in Paris, St. Amable in Montreal, the Laurel Point Inn in Victoria, La Trattoria di Umberto in Whistler, and many more, along the way earning the title of Maître Artisan. Recently, he worked at Government House in British Columbia for the Lieutenant-Governor, the Honourable Steven L. Point, cooking for Prince Charles of Wales and the Duchess of Cornwall.

He is now relishing the abundance of local produce and fresh berries available in the Thompson Canyon area. He is the new chef at the Cutting Board Restaurant at the Kumsheen Rafting Resort in Lytton, BC, where he is keeping busy discovering and creating new ways to introduce native ingredients into his menu.

Blackberry Crumble with Jalapeno Honey Butter

Makes 4 servings

½ cup (125 mL) flour

¼ cup (60 mL) brown sugar

⅔ cup (160 mL) unsalted butter, divided

¼ cup (60 mL) rolled oats

1 cup (250 mL) fresh or frozen blackberries

¼ cup (60 mL) white sugar

2 Tbsp (30 mL) honey

1 small jalapeno pepper, seeds removed and diced finely

After a morning spent picking blackberries in your favourite secret berry patch, what better use of the berries than this dessert? If you want a more traditional approach, replace the jalapeno honey butter with ice cream or whipped cream.

1. Preheat the oven to 350°F (180°C).

2. In a large bowl, mix together flour and brown sugar. Rub in 4 tablespoons (60 mL) of the butter until mixture resembles coarse breadcrumbs, then stir in rolled oats.

3. Divide blackberries among 4 ramekin dishes, or 1 large dish, and sprinkle white sugar over the top.

4. Cover berries with crumble mixture and pat gently—not too hard!

5. Place on baking sheet and bake for 20 minutes for ramekins and 30 minutes for large-sized crumble.

6. Place honey and jalapeno pepper in a small saucepan and bring to a very gentle simmer for 2 minutes. Remove from heat and allow to cool before stirring in remaining 7 tablespoons (100 mL) of soft, but not melted, butter.

7. When crumble comes out of the oven, allow to cool for a few minutes, then serve with jalapeno honey butter on the side.

Dark Chocolate French Toast with Summer Berries

Makes 4 servings

This healthy breakfast is cleverly disguised as a dessert. It's a great recipe to make with your kids because they'll love dunking the bread in the mixture and making a mess. Don't be afraid to get your hands dirty!

1. Under gently running water, wash fresh berries, and slice strawberries if using.

2. Spread lemon curd on one side of all the slices of bread.

3. Cover 4 of the slices with mixed berries, saving a few for garnish.

4. Top with second slice of bread, curd side in, and trim crusts if desired.

5. In a large bowl, whisk eggs, cream, milk, and cocoa vigorously, then dip each sandwich into the mix, soaking for at least a minute.

6. Warm a heavy frying pan over medium heat, then add half of the clarified butter. Cook 2 sandwiches at a time until golden brown and crispy on both sides. (Sandwiches may be placed on a baking sheet and finished in the oven if bread is especially thick.)

7. Slice each sandwich into 4 triangles and garnish with a few fresh berries and a dusting of icing sugar.

Chef's Tip: Use strawberries, blueberries, blackberries, loganberries, etc. Fresh berries are much better for texture, but you can also use frozen.

1½ cup (375 mL) summer berries (see Chef's Tip)

½ cup (125 mL) Lemon Curd (p. 19)

8 slices whole wheat bread

3 eggs

½ cup (125 mL) whipping cream

½ cup (125 mL) milk

2 Tbsp (30 mL) cocoa powder

¼ cup (60 mL) clarified butter, divided (see Chef's Tip, p. 12)

2 tsp (10 mL) icing sugar, for dusting

Crabapple and Pecan Tarte Tatin with Lavender Crème Anglaise

Chef Chance Wilke

Makes a 12-inch (30 cm) tart, or four 4-inch (10 cm) individual tarts

Tart

1 cup (250 mL) cake flour

1 cup (250 mL) all-purpose flour

½ tsp (2 mL) salt

¾ cup (185 mL) cold butter, cubed

2 eggs

18–20 small crabapples

1¼ cups (310 mL) sugar

1¼ cups (310 mL) butter

1 cup (250 mL) pecan pieces

Lavender Crème Anglaise

1½ cups (375 mL) milk

half a vanilla bean

1 Tbsp (15 mL) lavender, fresh or dried

4 egg yolks

½ cup (125 mL) sugar

Chef's Tip: With tarts and pies, always preheat the oven to 400°F (200°C), then start preparing the dough to allow it time to rest; it's best rolled out practically frozen.

Crabapples are usually seen as somewhat of a nuisance, falling all over the place and being too bitter to eat. This recipe gives them a full makeover, and you won't even recognize them when they're all dressed up!

Tart

1. Sift together cake flour and all-purpose flour, then add salt. On a clean surface, scoop the flour and form a well in the middle. Place butter and eggs into the well. With a pastry cutter, cut together butter and flour until butter is smaller than the size of a pea with no loose flour left. Do not overmix or gluten will form, which is not what you want. If the dough can't hold together, add 2 tsp (10 mL) cold water. Press dough into a ball and flatten, wrap in plastic, and place in the fridge or freezer to rest.

2. Find a 12-inch (30 cm) serving plate that can also double as a trace for the tart dough. (If making 4-inch [10 cm] tarts, most sugar bowls and coffee mugs are approximately 4 inches [10 cm] in diameter at their mouth and can be used as the trace.)

3. Peel and core crabapples, then slice them.

4. In a large frying pan, start melting sugar and butter, and then add pecans. Place two-thirds of the crabapples in the pan in a neat circle, adding more apples as they cook down and shrink.

5. Once apples are soft and sugar is starting to brown, roll out tart dough until 2 inches (5 cm) thick, cut pastry into a circle, and place over the top of the apples in the pan.

6. Bake for 18–20 minutes at 400°F (200°C), allowing the crust to brown. Remove from the oven and allow to cool, then refrigerate overnight to let the apples set.

Crème Anglaise

1. In a medium pot, heat milk, lavender, and vanilla bean, and bring to a boil (steeping the lavender brings out more flavour).

2. In a stainless steel bowl, whip egg yolks and sugar, then slowly add the infused hot milk to the bowl while continuing to stir the mixture. Return the mixture to the pot and cook over low heat. Allow sauce to cook and thicken. (A good way to tell if the sauce is done is to place a wooden spoon in the pot and swipe a finger across; if it doesn't run, it's finished.)

3. Cool and refrigerate.

4. To serve, place the frying pan in a 350°F (160°C) oven to warm the tart. Once warm, place the serving plate over the top of the pan and flip it over so that the tart lands on the plate.

5. Cut into equal slices and serve with lavender crème anglaise and French vanilla ice cream.

Chef Chance Wilke likes to "kick it old skool" by making classic dishes with a local twist. He was born in Victoria but grew up all over Vancouver Island, where he derived his inspiration and love of local food. He received his Red Seal after graduating from Campbell River's Culinary College at the age of 23. Chance is a young, aspiring, hard-working chef with a promising career ahead of him. He's worked as an apprentice in Victoria, and as an executive chef in the Comox Valley. Currently, he lives in Victoria and hopes to open his own restaurant in the near future, basing the cuisine on the buy local motto.

Honey Pear Conserve

Nancy Brown, Farm Planner, Woodwynn Farms Therapeutic Community

Makes 4 pints (2 L)

5 cups (1.25 L) washed, cored, and chopped fresh pears

2 lemons, finely chopped and deseeded

1 orange, finely chopped and deseeded

2 cups (500 mL) raisins

3½ cups (875 mL) honey

This fresh and tasty pear conserve is lovely when served with pork or game, or on vanilla ice cream. All the fruit is left unpeeled in this recipe.

1. Place all of the ingredients in a large saucepan.
2. Cook over medium heat, stirring frequently until thick.
3. Let the mixture cool slightly, but pour into sterilized jars while still hot. Seal jars.

Chef's Tip: The pear conserve and the jars should both be hot when packed and sealed. Add a sprig of fresh mint when serving.

View of the Saanich Peninsula with Woodwynn Farms in the centre.

Detoxifying Tea

Nancy Brown, Farm Planner, Woodwynn Farms Therapeutic Community

Makes 1¾ cups (435 mL)

This tea clears and cleanses the liver and gallbladder from the effects of heavy meat, alcohol, and fat diets. The roots can be fresh or dried and are best for this particular tea when harvested in the fall.

¼ oz (7 g) dried dandelion root
¼ oz (7 g) dried burdock root
¼ oz (7 g) dried chicory root

1. Combine 2 cups (500 mL) cold water and dried roots in a large saucepan.
2. Place over medium heat and bring to a boil.
3. Cover and simmer for 20 minutes.
4. Strain and drink a glassful 3 times a day with meals.

Chef's Tip: These roots can all be sourced at the Woodwynn Farms market, which is open on Saturdays throughout the summer.

Nancy Brown grew up in a large family on the prairies of Montana and Alberta, where she learned the art of wildcrafting (also known as "harvesting from the land") and where she experienced the healing power of plants and nature. With a firm grounding in mothering (she has three sons), horticulture, ecology, environmental studies, farming, blacksmithing, art, and design, as well as a deep level of commitment and care to the power of healing through relationships, she has come to the Creating Homefulness Society project on Woodwynn Farms, where she acts as farm planner and project coordinator.

Summer Forest Wasabi Mojito

Edgar Smith, Beaver Meadow Farms, Comox Valley

Makes 1 serving

2 or 3 fresh wasabi leaves

2 or 3 fresh mint leaves

½ tsp (2 mL) brown sugar

2 oz (60 mL) white rum

enough ice to almost fill the glass

4 oz (125 mL) soda water

huckleberries or salmonberries,
for garnishing

Beaver Meadow Farms is the home of Natural Pastures Cheese and organic grass-fed Angus beef. After a hot summer's afternoon in the fields, it is wonderful to retreat to the shaded rainforest for a cool break and a favourite drink.

1. Under the cool canopy of Sitka spruce and western red cedar, among the devil's club and skunk cabbage, gather wasabi and mint leaves. Beware of sleeping bears.

2. From the cold, flowing spring, pull out a chilled glass, add wasabi and mint leaves to taste, and muddle with a blunted red cedar stick.

3. Add brown sugar and muddle some more.

4. Add white rum, ice, and soda. Garnish with some huckleberries or salmonberries.

5. Find a soft, mossy stump, sit, and enjoy the evening forest. Repeat as necessary. Put the glass, rum, and soda back in the spring for next time.

The Smith Family started Beaver Meadow Farms in the mid-1930s, and family members continue to farm the land today. Beaver Meadows is a certified Heritage Dairy Farm, using only natural systems of farming. The farm meets and exceeds standards for the ethical treatment of animals, biodiversity, and pesticide-free farming practices. Beaver Meadow Farms also runs and operates Natural Pastures Cheese, an award-winning specialty artisan fromagerie, and Natural Pastures Beef, which raises organic, grass-fed beef.

A perfect spot to sip Summer Forest Mojitos .

River and

There is a traditional First Nations saying that goes, "When the tide is out, dinner is served."

We are blessed on the West Coast to have an abundance of amazing food in our rivers and seas. These tasty and nutritious treasures are plentiful due to the clean and healthy waters along our coastline.

We have so much choice, including our iconic wild, rich salmon; delicious, firm halibut; sweet, juicy crab; plump mussels; giant oysters; meaty scallops, clams, and shrimp; and our wonderful spot prawns that everyone loves. The recipes in this section will hopefully give you both traditional and new ways to enjoy this wonderful seafood.

Sea

Ultimate West Coast Seafood Eggs Benedict

Clair Oates, Clair's B & B, Ladner

Makes 1 serving (but can be scaled easily)

1 English muffin half

1 Tbsp (15 mL) smoked salmon cream cheese

1 Tbsp (15 mL) Dungeness crabmeat

1 thick slice heirloom tomato

sea salt, ground pepper, and olive oil, to taste

3 oz (90 g) sockeye salmon fillet

light canola oil, for frying

1 large spot prawn, peeled and deveined, tail on

1/3 tsp (1.75 mL) white vinegar

1 large egg

2 lox salmon slices, for garnishing

5 asparagus spears (or sea asparagus), for garnishing

1/3 cup (80 mL) hollandaise sauce (storebought, or p. 12)

6 capers, for garnishing (optional)

1 lemon wedge, for garnishing (optional)

Believe it or not, this is an easy, quick, yet impressive breakfast. You can make it all from scratch, or you can use a few shortcuts!

1. Set out on a baking sheet as many English muffins halves as you have guests.

2. Spread each half with cream cheese, then top with crabmeat and tomato slice. Season with sea salt, fresh ground pepper, and olive oil.

3. Place in a 400°F (200°C) oven for 10 minutes before serving.

4. Season prepared salmon fillet(s) lightly with sea salt and pepper, then place skin side down in a hot sauté pan prepared with canola oil. Brown skin until crispy, then turn over and finish cooking for 2 minutes. Do not overcook, just warm and crisp.

5. Remove salmon fillet(s) from the pan and let rest in a warm oven until ready to plate.

6. In the same sauté pan, cook prepared spot prawn(s) quickly for approximately 2 minutes per side. Place prawn(s) on 3-inch (8 cm) toothpick(s) and keep warm for plating.

7. Fill a low-sided pot or pan with enough water to cover the top of egg(s). Add vinegar. Bring water to a rapid boil, then turn down to a gentle simmer. Stir water to get a current going around the pot and gently break in egg(s), allowing water to swirl around.

8. Let egg(s) rest in simmering water for 2 minutes then gently slip a spatula underneath to release from the pan bottom. Cook to the hardness preference of your guests (the longer the simmer, the harder the egg).

9. To serve, artfully spread lox salmon slices and asparagus on a warmed plate.

10. Add English muffin to the plate and top with sautéed salmon and poached egg (this may be a bit of a balancing act!).

11. Pour hollandaise sauce over the top and garnish with the prawned toothpick to hold everything together.

12. If you wish, sprinkle with capers and serve with a wedge of fresh lemon.

Chef's Tip: Raid your garden for a flower to finish your presentation (nasturtiums look great). Other great garnishes are sea asparagus or asparagus tips.

Clair Oates learned to cook her amazing seafood dishes on a wood stove (at her mother's knee) on Bath Island, a twelve-acre island in the Strait of Georgia. After years of summer jobs, commercial fishing with her father, and working in the kitchens of local resorts, she swam away from home to spend two summers cooking in Jasper National Park. Clair now owns and runs Clair's Bed and Breakfast in the fishing and farming village of Ladner, BC. Clair loves welcoming guests from around the world to her art deco–inspired home and preparing wonderful dishes to tempt the palate.

Rocky Mountaineer Wild Pacific Sockeye Salmon

Executive Chef Frédéric Couton, Rocky Mountaineer

Makes 4 servings

8 unpeeled baby red potatoes
(about 2 cups/500 mL)

vegetable oil, for roasting

salt and pepper, to taste

¼ cup (60 mL) shaved fennel

10 drops lemon juice

4 8 oz (250 g) portions sockeye
salmon, boneless and skin on

½ tsp (2 mL) smoked sea salt

1 cup (250 mL) assorted fresh
vegetables, trimmed (see Chef's Tip)

olive oil, for frying

2 Tbsp (30 mL) grainy mustard

1 Tbsp (15 mL) white wine vinegar

¼ cup (60 mL) olive oil

1 sprig dill (or sprouts), for garnishing

Chef's Tip: Use vegetables such as
carrots, asparagus, broccoli, red peppers, zucchini, or peas.

One of Rocky Mountaineer's most popular dishes, this West Coast creation combines the best of both land and sea. Wild Pacific salmon is creatively stacked on a bed of fresh sautéed vegetables and tender nugget potatoes, and artistically finished with delectable fennel slaw and a drizzle of old-fashioned mustard vinaigrette.

1. Roast potatoes in the oven at 375°F (180°C) drizzled with vegetable oil, until cooked (20–25 minutes, depending on the size of the potatoes), then season with salt and pepper.

2. "Shave" fennel by slicing it paper thin using a very sharp knife, then add lemon juice to prevent oxidation.

3. Pan-fry salmon skin side down until lightly seared, and finish in the oven at 350°F (190°C) for 8 minutes.

4. In a pan over medium heat, sauté vegetables in olive oil and season with salt and pepper.

5. Prepare vinaigrette by mixing together mustard, vinegar, and olive oil (see p. 6 for directions).

6. To serve, plate vegetables and potatoes and top with salmon and shaved fennel. Drizzle vinaigrette all over the plate.

This recipe appears on the front cover.

Born in the French Alps, **Frédéric Couton** trained at Michelin-starred restaurants, honing his culinary skills in the kitchens of Hilton hotels in Paris and Geneva. He continued to pursue his career in Montreal, Bangkok, and Vancouver, where he held the position of executive chef at the prestigious British Columbia Club before joining the Cannery Seafood House in 1996. Couton has won many international awards in culinary competitions at home and abroad. His latest achievement is a masterpiece cookbook, *The Cannery Seafood House Cookbook*, published in 2006.

Cedar Wrapped Salmon with Peppered Oysters and Red Pepper Salsa

Makes 4 servings

Salmon

4 cedar sheets (or use 1 cedar plank)

4 oysters

4 tsp (20 mL) fresh cracked peppercorns, to taste

4 5 oz (150 g) salmon fillets, cleaned and pin bones removed

2 tsp (10 mL) sea salt

This salmon came all dressed up for the party, and it will be a hit at yours! Whether you choose to serve the fish wrapped in cedar, or lined up in a row on a cedar plank, its elegant presentation will turn heads.

Salmon

1. Soak cedar sheets or plank in water for at least 2 hours before using.

2. Preheat the oven to 350°F (180°C) if using cedar sheets or to 325°F (160°C) if using a cedar plank; alternately, set barbecue temperature to medium-high.

3. Shuck oysters and reserve liquid.

4. Pat oysters dry and lightly roll in cracked peppercorns.

5. One at a time, place each salmon fillet at the front of a cedar sheet and brush with reserved oyster liquid. Season with a little sea salt and place 1 peppered oyster on top. Roll up cedar sheet quite tightly so that the seam runs along the bottom of the roll. Alternately, create a row of oyster-topped salmon fillets on the cedar plank.

6. Place onto a baking sheet and cook for 10–15 minutes depending on the size of the fillets. Salmon should be cooked to medium doneness with a nice little bit of pink in the centre.

Salsa

1. While salmon is cooking, combine salsa ingredients together.
2. Serve salmon and oysters on cedar sheets for individual plates, or on the plank for the table, with red pepper salsa on the side.

Chef's Tip: You can find cedar sheets at some supermarkets and at specialty fishmongers and food stores.

Salsa

1 small red pepper, finely diced

1 small red onion, finely diced

2 tsp (10 mL) finely chopped fresh cilantro

3 Tbsp (45 mL) olive oil

salt and pepper, to taste

West coast rollers at Port Renfrew Beach.

Dayboat Halibut with Grainy Mustard Spaetzle and Ragout of Bacon and Peas

Executive Chef Alex Tung, Yowza!culinary + concepts

Makes 2 servings

Halibut

2 Tbsp (30 mL) grapeseed oil

6 oz (175 g) halibut fillet, boneless and skinless

sea salt, to taste

1 garlic clove, crushed

1 thyme sprig, crushed

1 Tbsp (15 mL) unsalted butter

Mustard Spaetzle

3 eggs

¾ cup plus 1 Tbsp (200 mL) homogenized milk

2 Tbsp (30 mL) grainy mustard

1 cup (250 mL) all-purpose flour

nutmeg, to taste

sea salt and pepper, to taste

2 Tbsp (30 mL) grapeseed oil, divided

1 Tbsp (15 mL) butter

1 Tbsp (15 mL) finely chopped chives

Halibut has quite the past. Its name is derived from *haly* ("holy") and *butt* ("flat fish"), so called due to its popularity on Catholic holy days. Halibut is still a West Coast favourite that has Chef Tung eagerly awaiting halibut season each year.

Halibut

1. Preheat the oven to 350°F (180°C).

2. Heat a non-stick pan over medium-high, then add grapeseed oil.

3. Season halibut with salt and place presentation side down in the pan.

4. Allow fish to sear and brown gently, then place crushed garlic clove and thyme in the pan to perfume the oil.

5. Turn over the fish gently when nicely browned, then add butter to the pan and baste fish with browned butter.

6. Remove halibut from pan and place on a parchment-lined pan to finish cooking in the oven while you prepare the spaetzle and ragout. Halibut is done when it starts to flake; the centre of the fillet should still be slightly opaque, but warm.

Mustard Spaetzle

1. In a large bowl, mix eggs, milk, and grainy mustard, then sift in flour and incorporate gently.

2. Season with nutmeg, salt, and pepper.

3. Using a dough scraper, push batter through a perforated pan or cheese grater into a pot of rapidly boiling salted water.

4. Drain and dry spaetzle on a paper towel, coat lightly with oil, and then let cool.

5. Heat a frying pan over medium-high; add remaining grapeseed oil and a layer of spaetzle.

6. Allow spaetzle to brown, then sauté and allow other side to brown.

7. Add butter to the pan, allowing it to melt but not burn, and finish with additional seasoning and chives. Set aside while you prepare the ragout.

Ragout

1. Heat a frying pan over medium, add oil, and lightly sauté bacon, peas, onions, and mushrooms.

2. When warmed through, add tomatoes, butter, and red wine sauce.

3. Adjust seasoning to your taste and finish with chives.

4. To assemble the dish, place browned spaetzle in the centre of each plate, spoon warm ragout over the top, and add half of the perfectly cooked halibut. Finish with a gentle drizzle of good-quality olive oil.

Ragout

1 Tbsp (15 mL) grapeseed oil

1 Tbsp (15 mL) double-smoked bacon, rendered (cooked until the fat runs out)

1 Tbsp (15 mL) freshly shucked peas

3 pearl onions, blanched

2 shiitake mushrooms, thinly sliced

3 grape tomatoes, halved

1 Tbsp (15 mL) butter

1 Tbsp (15 mL) red wine sauce or demi-glace (homemade or storebought)

sea salt and pepper, to taste

1 Tbsp (15 mL) finely chopped chives

Having cooked in some of the top kitchens around the world and won many culinary awards, **Chef Alex Tung** is now the owner/executive chef of Yowza!culinary + concepts, a boutique firm focused on restaurant consulting, culinary media, and distinctive catering. His passion for restaurants, pervasive financial background, innovative marketing strategy, and enthusiastic approach to cuisine lend themselves well to developing his culinary consultancy.

Steamed Halibut Fillet on Spanish Chorizo, Leeks, and Cherry Tomatoes

Gilbert Noussitou, Camosun College

Makes 4 servings

4 Tbsp (60 mL) olive oil

1 cup (250 mL) sliced leeks

4 Tbsp (60 mL) julienned red pepper

3 oz (90 g) chorizo sausage, cut into small pieces

⅛ tsp (1 mL) smoked paprika (hot)

20 cherry tomatoes

2½ cups (625 mL) chicken stock (or vegetable or fish stock)

2 tsp (10 mL) lemon juice

salt and freshly ground black pepper, to taste

½ Tbsp (7.5 mL) chives, chopped, divided

4 5 oz (150 g) skinless halibut fillets

Some like it hot! Hot paprika and spicy chorizo sausage give this little halibut a kick.

1. Heat olive oil in a small saucepan, then add leeks and sweat them until translucent.

2. Add red pepper and chorizo, and sauté until sausage starts changing colour.

3. Add paprika and sauté lightly.

4. Add cherry tomatoes, chicken stock, and lemon juice; bring to a simmer.

5. Season to taste with salt and pepper, then simmer gently for 2 minutes.

6. Stir in half of the chives and place halibut fillets on top. Season with salt and pepper, then cover and reduce heat to very low. Let halibut steam for about 5 minutes; do not lift the lid.

7. When halibut is cooked, place a quarter of the sauce onto each plate, then top with steamed halibut, and garnish with remaining chives.

A graduate of École Hôtelière des Pyrénées in Toulouse, France, **Gilbert Noussitou** has been practising his trade for 38 years in some of the finest establishments of France, England, and Canada. His varied experience includes winning national and international awards, owning a restaurant, a catering company, and sharing his expertise as a consultant. Gilbert is a certified chef de cuisine and a diploma instructor at Camosun College, which he joined in 1988 and where he currently chairs the Culinary Arts Program. Over the years, Gilbert has often taken a leadership role for many committees, community events, and professional associations, including the BC Restaurant and Foodservices Association, the BC Agri-Tourism Alliance, the Canadian Culinary Federation, the Society of Vocational Instructors of BC, and many more.

The Cowichan River.

Ginger Beer Braised Halibut with Oven Baked Yam Fries and Tartar Sauce

Makes 4 servings

Fish 'n' Chips

2 medium yams
salt and pepper
2 Tbsp (30 mL) vegetable oil
4 5 oz (150 g) skinless halibut fillets
11 oz (330 mL) bottle ginger beer

Tartar Sauce

⅓ cup plus 1 Tbsp (100 mL)
mayonnaise (p. 8)
3 Tbsp (45 mL) sour cream
1 Tbsp (15 mL) chopped capers
1 tsp (5 mL) chopped fresh dill
1 Tbsp (15 mL) chopped gherkins

Chef's Tip: For extra zip, add a squeeze of lemon or some cayenne pepper to the tartar sauce.

This is a really healthy way to enjoy your fish 'n' chips—all the taste but far fewer calories!

Fish 'n' Chips

1. Preheat the oven to 400°F (200°C).
2. Scrub yams well and slice into fries approximately ½ inch × ½ inch × 3 inches (1 cm × 1 cm × 8 cm). (If thicker fries are desired, just increase cooking time.)
3. Add fries to a large bowl, sprinkle with salt and pepper and vegetable oil, then toss thoroughly to coat well.
4. Spread yams on parchment-lined baking sheet and bake for 20–25 minutes. Turn occasionally to ensure even browning.
5. Cut a circle of parchment paper to fit and line the bottom of a heavy-based frying pan, then heat pan over medium-high (if parchment browns quickly, reduce heat).
6. Season halibut with salt and pepper. Add just enough oil to the pan to lubricate the parchment paper and add halibut fillets presentation side down.
7. Cook for 1–2 minutes only, then flip and cook for 30 seconds more before sliding paper out from under halibut fillets. Set parchment paper aside.
8. Add ginger beer to the pan, then place halibut in the beer with the parchment paper on top. Reduce the heat to very low and cook for 6–8 minutes, depending on fillet thickness.

Tartar Sauce

1. Prepare the tartar sauce by mixing together mayonnaise, sour cream, capers, dill, gherkins, and a pinch of salt and pepper. Place sauce in a communal bowl, or serve in 4 individual bowls if preferred.

Crispy Dogfish and Mushy Peas

Chef Dan Hayes, The London Chef, Victoria

Makes 6 servings

Fish

1 medium or 2 small
dogfish fillets, skinless

½ cup (125 mL) all-purpose flour

2 eggs, beaten with a splash of milk

2 cups (500 mL) panko breadcrumbs

canola oil, for deep-frying
(see Chef's Tip)

flaked sea salt, to taste

freshly ground black pepper, to taste

Peas

1 small white onion, chopped

3 Tbsp (45 mL) unsalted
butter, divided

sea salt

3 cups (750 mL) fresh or frozen peas

1 cup (250 mL) chicken stock

2 fresh mint sprigs

Dogfish has never been taken seriously. It's an ugly, scaly fish that is quite often an accidental bycatch that is discarded as trash or thrown overboard dead. This is wasteful and unsustainable, so don't follow the crowd: when prepared properly, dogfish is amazingly delicious. Mushy peas are a traditional accompaniment to fried fish in Northern England.

Fish

1. Cut dogfish fillets into bite-sized pieces (*goujons*). Set flour, beaten eggs, and panko in separate bowls and dredge goujons first in flour, then in egg, and finally, in panko, pressing the breadcrumbs firmly onto the fish to coat fillets thoroughly.

2. Heat canola oil in a deep fryer to 350°F (180°F), then fry goujons in small batches until golden brown.

3. Drain fried fish on a paper towel, then season heavily with sea salt and a pinch of fresh black pepper.

Peas

1. In a saucepan, over a low temperature, sweat chopped onion in 2 Tbsp (30 mL) butter and season with salt. After 4–5 minutes, add peas, chicken stock, and mint.

2. Bring to a slight simmer for about 2 minutes. (You don't want to overcook the peas or they will lose their colour.) Drain and discard half the liquid and remove the mint sprigs. Remove and roughly chop the mint leaves.

3. In a food processor, blend peas, remaining cooking liquid, mint leaves, and 1 Tbsp (15 mL) butter. Blend until smooth, and serve warm or at room temperature.

Chef's Tip: If you don't have a deep fryer at home, you can heat the oil to 350°F (180°C) in a saucepan. Be sure you have a proper thermometer because this temperature ensures the fish will crisp nicely and cook thoroughly.

Chef's Tip: Serve the dogfish with tartar sauce for dipping (p. 11 or p. 63).

Chef Dan Hayes and his wife, **Micayla**, are the perfectly matched team behind The London Chef. Micayla brings strong business acumen to the table, and Dan brings unparalleled culinary ability. From commis to head chef, Dan has worked with various talented chefs in numerous high-end and Michelin-starred restaurants. He has taught cookery all over the UK, food styled with one of Britain's top food photography companies, and consulted on the development and opening of restaurants in London and the Canary Islands. From fishing, hunting, and gathering to final presentation, Dan combines his classical French training with his love of rustic Mediterranean cuisine and seafood cookery to create memorable and outstanding dishes, events, and cookery lessons.

Rainbow Trout with Raspberries

Christoph Luther, Owner, The Logpile Lodge, Smithers

Makes 4 servings

4 10–12 oz (300–400 g) whole fresh rainbow trout

flour, for coating fish

¼ cup (60 mL) sunflower oil

3.5 oz (100 g) butter (clarified if preferred), divided

1 large shallot, diced

12 leaves fresh sage

salt and pepper, to taste

1 cup (250 mL) fresh raspberries

Smithers has something of a reputation for its trout and deservedly so. We caught our trout fresh on Chapman Lake, but if fishing isn't your thing, cast a reel at your local grocers to find this flavourful fish. Serve with basmati rice or pan-fried potatoes with apples.

1. Clean trout and use scissors to remove bones behind heads and in front of tails.

2. Dredge trout in flour to coat them nicely.

3. Using 1 or 2 frying pans, heat oil and fry trout on both sides. (Fish is cooked when the fins separate easily.) Keep warm.

4. In a frying pan, warm 1 ounce (30 g) butter over medium heat (butter shouldn't brown), then add shallot and stir until pieces look glassy, then add sage and stir until leaves are crispy but still greenish in colour. Add remaining butter and let melt.

5. Prepare fish by peeling off the skin and slicing down the middle of each side to produce 4 half-fillets; arrange pieces on a plate in a flower-like pattern.

6. Reheat butter sauce and add salt, pepper, and raspberries. Heat raspberry sauce until it starts to lightly brown, then spoon carefully over the top of the fish.

After immigrating to Canada from Switzerland in 1993, **Christoph and Barbara Luther** built their dream just outside of Smithers: The Logpile Lodge, a gorgeous log building hosting seven guestrooms and a dining room. After three years of building the lodge, Christoph traded in hammer and chainsaw for apron and whisk and started the Logpile Lodge Restaurant with Barbara. Over the past 14 years, Chris has combined traditional dishes and new flavours with funky ingredients, never forgetting the ever-so-important butter, cream, cheese, and chocolate (he can't deny his Swiss roots!).

Trout fresh from Chapman Lake.

Soft Jalapeno Crab Tacos with Tomato Chutney

Makes 12 tacos

Taco night just got a tasty West Coast facelift!

Tomato Chutney

1. In a small pan, combine all chutney ingredients and cook over medium heat for 30 minutes, or until thick and syrupy. Remove from heat and allow to cool.

Tacos

1. Wrap tortillas in foil and warm in the oven for 10 minutes while you prepare crabmeat filling.

2. Meanwhile, warm a frying pan over moderate heat, then add oil and sauté garlic, onion, and jalapeno lightly. Remove from heat and add crabmeat and cilantro.

3. Place one-twelfth of the crab filling onto each warm tortilla, cover with a spoonful of chutney, and finish with a pinch of spinach and a lemon wedge.

Chef's Tip: To avoid a mess when you're eating, try folding in one end of the taco. But if you still make a mess, laugh about it, and continue eating!

Tomato Chutney

2 large heirloom tomatoes, diced

1 medium onion, diced

3 cloves garlic, minced

2 Tbsp (30 mL) brown sugar

2 Tbsp (30 mL) white vinegar

salt and pepper, to taste

Tacos

12 6-inch (15 cm) corn tortillas

2 Tbsp (30 mL) olive oil

1 clove garlic, minced or pressed

1 small red onion, finely chopped

1 small jalapeno chili, diced

1 lb (500 g) shelled
and cooked crabmeat

half a bunch cilantro, chopped coarsely

1 small bunch spinach, shredded

12 lemon wedges, for garnishing

Cow Bay Café Crab Cakes with Creole Tomato Glaze

Adrienne Johnston, Owner, Cow Bay Café, Prince Rupert

from *No More Secrets: Recipes from the Cow Bay Café*

Makes 8 servings (depending on size of crabs)

3–4 Tbsp (45–60 mL) kosher salt

3 large Dungeness crabs, shelled, halved, and ready to cook

¾ cup (185 mL) mayonnaise (p. 8)

3 Tbsp (45 mL) green Tabasco sauce

1 large red pepper, diced

half a yellow pepper, diced

half an orange pepper, diced

half a medium red onion, diced

¼ cup (60 mL) fresh parsley, minced

¼ cup (60 mL) fresh dill

¼ cup (60 mL) fresh tarragon

¼ cup (60 mL) fresh basil, minced (see Chef's Tip)

4–6½ cups (1–1.5 L) breadcrumbs, fresh and soft, divided (see Chef's Tip)

vegetable oil, for frying

Adrienne's crab cakes are something of a legend: with fresh crab pulled straight from the ocean at Prince Rupert, and her excellent recipe, they really are special. We are thrilled to be able to include her recipe in this book.

1. Fill a large stockpot about one-third full with water and add salt. Put a lid on it and set the heat to high, so the water comes to a boil as fast as possible.

2. When salted water is boiling, add as much of the crab as possible, but be sure that the lid still fits snugly on the pot. Return the water to a boil and then start timing. All the crab should be exposed to the hot steam, but the pot should not boil over. (The heat and lid may have to be adjusted.)

3. After 15 minutes, drain, cool, and shuck the crab into big chunks. Refrigerate while preparing remaining ingredients as cooked crab deteriorates quickly.

4. Mix together mayonnaise and Tabasco sauce.

5. In a large bowl, combine diced peppers and onion, herbs, and 2½ cups (625 mL) of the breadcrumbs. Add mayonnaise mixture and mix gently but thoroughly. Add crab and mix again gently and thoroughly to keep chunks as intact as possible.

6. Form into balls about the size of billiard balls. If you weigh the first few, you will find they should weigh 3½–4 ounces (100–140 grams).

7. Flatten each ball into a cake about ¾ inch (2 cm) thick. Dredge crab cakes in remaining breadcrumbs before frying in vegetable oil over medium heat to a nice brown colour and heated all the way through.

8. Serve with Creole Tomato Glaze (p. 72).

Chef's Tip: If available, use a combination of Thai basil and regular basil.

Chef's Tip: It is fine to use a food processor for mincing the herbs, but don't wash it out until you have finished making the soft breadcrumbs, as the crumbs will absorb any herbs remaining in the food processor.

Adrienne Johnston was born in India and raised all over the world. Her family have always been the best fans of her cooking. She loves being in Prince Rupert where she has lived for the last 35 years. Having worked in nursing and as a children's librarian, she finds cooking and running a restaurant has been the most rewarding of all her careers. Respect for food, farmers, fisherman, grape growers, winemakers, and purveyors of all of the aforementioned drives her own passion for cooking. She has just released her first cookery book: *No More Secrets: Recipes from the Cow Bay Café*.

Creole Tomato Glaze

Makes 2 cups (500 mL)

1 cup (250 mL) white sugar

¼ cup (60 mL) Louisiana hot sauce

¼ cup (60 mL) apple cider vinegar

2½ Tbsp (37.5 mL) tomato paste

2 tsp (10 mL) smooth Dijon mustard

1 Tbsp (15 mL) kosher salt

1 tsp (5 mL) garlic powder

½ tsp (2 mL) finely
ground black pepper

¼ tsp (1 mL) celery salt

2 fresh or dried bay leaves

1. In a medium saucepan over medium heat, combine all ingredients.

2. Whisk to combine and dissolve the sugar, bring to a boil, and cook for 3 minutes.

3. Remove from heat, strain, and cool. This sauce will keep for a couple of weeks in the fridge.

Waterfalls at Puntledge
River near Courtenay

Crabby Rice Cakes with Berry Vinaigrette

Makes 4 servings

¼ cup (60 mL) sushi rice

11 oz (330 mL) can coconut milk

2 tsp (10 mL) hot sauce

salt and pepper, to taste

½ lb (250 g) Dungeness crab, shelled and cleaned

½ cup (125 mL) blackberries, strawberries, raspberries, etc.

1 tsp (5 mL) honey

1 Tbsp (15 mL) rice wine vinegar

¼ cup (60 mL) vegetable oil, plus additional oil for frying

¼ cup (60 mL) whole blackberries, strawberries, raspberries, for garnishing

Another delicious version of crab cakes, but this one is good for those on a gluten-free diet.

1. Add rice, coconut milk, and hot sauce to a small pan, then add a pinch of salt and pepper. Bring to a simmer over moderate heat, stirring frequently.

2. Once mixture is simmering, cover with a tight-fitting lid and reduce heat to low. Cook for 10 minutes, then remove from heat *but do not* remove lid or even look inside.

3. Allow to cool for about 20 minutes, then remove the lid and fluff rice with a fork before mixing in crabmeat.

4. Firmly pack mixture into an ice cream scoop, or shape by hand, to form 8 patties or croquette shapes. Allow to cool completely. Do not cover!

5. While crab cakes are cooling, prepare the berry vinaigrette. Over a small bowl, press berries through a fine sieve with the back of a spoon or spatula, then whisk together with honey and vinegar.

6. Slowly add all the oil to the bowl, whisking continuously. Taste, then adjust seasoning with salt and pepper.

7. Warm a non-stick frying pan over moderate heat and add enough oil to lightly coat the bottom. Add crab cakes and cook for 3–4 minutes until bottom is crisp and golden brown. Gently turn over and cook the other side until golden brown. (If crab cakes are large, you may need to place them on a baking sheet and finish them in the oven in order to heat them thoroughly but not burn them.)

8. Place 2 crab cakes on each plate, drizzle them with vinaigrette, and garnish with a few whole fresh berries.

Cortes Island Honey Mussels Cooked in Spinnakers Über Blonde Ale with Rouille

Chef Ali Ryan, Spinnakers Gastro Brewpub, Victoria

Makes 4 servings.

Mussels

60–64 honey mussels (see Chef's Tip)

1 bulb garlic

1 medium onion

olive oil

1 bottle Spinnakers Über Blonde Ale
(see Chef's Tip)

salt and pepper, to taste

2 sprigs parsley, finely
diced, for garnishing

Rouille

2 cloves garlic, crushed

pinch saffron threads

7 oz (200 g) jar roasted
red peppers, rinsed

2 Tbsp (30 mL) reduced-fat
mayonnaise

½ tsp salt

⅛ tsp cayenne pepper

This is a simple and delicious way to celebrate living on the Wet Coast: shellfish and craft-brewed beer! Serve mussels with warmed focaccia, sourdough, or french fries and rouille.

Mussels

1. Clean mussels by removing their beards. (This is easily done by gently holding the mussel in your hand and firmly pulling the beard out.) Discard any mussels with broken or cracked shells, and any that are already open.

2. Remove some of the loose layers of skin from the garlic bulb and slice off the top to expose the tops of the individual garlic cloves, then drizzle with a bit of olive oil and wrap tightly in foil. Roast in a 400°F (200°C) oven for 30–40 minutes. (Garlic is done when it feels soft when you squeeze the bulb.)

3. Slice onion thinly and set aside (the amount is up to your taste but a couple of slices per person is usually more than enough).

4. Find a pot large enough to comfortably fit mussels so they are not too piled on top of each other and in close proximity to the bottom of the pot. Warm pot over medium heat and add enough olive oil to lightly coat the bottom. Wait a moment for oil to heat up and then add onion slices.

Cont. on p. 78.

5. Once onion just begins to colour, squeeze some roasted garlic out of the cloves and add it to the pot. (Again, the amount is up to you but roasted garlic is sweet and sticky so you can be more liberal with it than raw garlic; try 2 or 3 cloves per person.) Stir onions and garlic together.

6. Open a bottle of Spinnakers Über Blonde Ale and pour yourself a taste to appreciate the delicious yeasty, malty flavours.

7. Add cleaned mussels to the onion–garlic mix, then quickly add just enough beer to cover them; initially, it will be quite foamy. Bring beer to a boil, then turn down the heat to maintain a vigorous simmer. (At this point, you are pretty much done; so, if you are lucky enough to only be cooking for yourself and a few others, this is when you enjoy the rest of the beer.)

Sea lions.

8. As mussels cook, they will open and release their juices. This salty liquid will combine and reduce down with the sweet, malty beer to create a surprisingly elegant sauce. Mussels are done when they are all fully open and the meat has lost its opaqueness and is brightly coloured. (Toss out any unopened mussels and don't try to force them open—you *really* don't want to know what a dead mussel looks and smells like.)

9. Taste broth and add salt and pepper as desired. Serve mussels in the broth with finely diced parsley sprinkled over the top.

Rouille

1. In a small saucepan, combine garlic, 1 tablespoon (15 mL) water, and saffron. Cover and cook over very low heat just until steaming, about 2 minutes.

2. Remove from heat and let stand for 2 minutes.

3. Combine garlic mixture, roasted red peppers, mayonnaise, salt, and cayenne in a blender or food processor; blend until smooth.

4. Transfer to a serving bowl and enjoy with your mussels!

Chef's Tip: Honey mussels can be found at many local fish markets. Smaller varieties can be used but the lovely plumpness of honeys can't be beat.

Chef's Tip: If you can't get your hands on Spinnakers Über Blonde Ale, you can substitute another Belgian ale. It's the Belgian yeast and malty flavours that are essential to this dish. Avoid any beer that is described as "hoppy" since hops are bitter by nature and become more so when reduced down.

Ali Ryan has been the chef at Spinnakers Gastro Brewpub for the past seven years. After moving from Ontario to Whistler, then on to Victoria after six years spent tree planting and cooking in bush camps, her love of good food, craft-brewed beer, and beautiful settings led her to Spinnakers. Ali and the Spinnakers team are dedicated to the local food movement and lessening their environmental footprint. Paul Hadfield, Spinnakers' owner, has been championing the local, sustainable food movement for decades. Spinnakers' kitchen now sources from more than 25 different Vancouver Island and BC-based small, artisan producers, including farmers, fisher people and seafood co-ops, ranchers, spice grinders, butchers, and cheese makers. The Spinnakers motto is "The heart of Spinnakers resides in the brewery and the soul in kitchen," and that pretty much says it all!

Fresh Wasabi Oysters on Short Grain Rice Cakes with Citrus and Wasabi Aïoli

Chef/Owner Ronald St. Pierre, Locals Restaurant, Courtenay

Makes 4 servings

This recipe combines some of the most West Coast ingredients you can get: beautiful local oysters and wasabi picked from the forest. Does it get any better than this?

Aïoli

3 egg yolks

2 Tbsp (30 mL) Dijon mustard

1 tsp (5 mL) sea salt

¾ tsp (4 mL) white pepper

1 Tbsp (15 mL) red wine vinegar

1 Tbsp (15 mL) lemon juice

3 Tbsp (45 mL) finely chopped lemon zest

3 Tbsp (45 mL) finely chopped roasted sweet red pepper

2 Tbsp (30 mL) julienned natural spring wasabi

1 Tbsp (15 mL) chopped fresh cilantro

4 cups (1 L) sunflower or canola oil

Ginger Marinade

4 Tbsp (60 mL) ginger

4 Tbsp (60 mL) garlic

⅓ cup (80 mL) soy sauce

2 oz (60 g) brown sugar

4 Tbsp (60 mL) organic pear juice

1 Tbsp (15 mL) sesame oil

2 Tbsp (30 mL) cilantro

1 tsp (5 mL) chili paste

1 Tbsp (15 mL) fresh lime juice

Aïoli

1. Place egg yolks, mustard, and salt in a blender; mix at medium speed.

2. Add remaining ingredients, except oil.

3. Add oil slowly to emulsify. Add a little cold water as needed to achieve desired consistency.

Ginger Marinade

1. Peel and slice ginger against the grain into small chunks.

2. Place all ingredients in a high-speed blender and mix until puréed.

Oysters

1. Shuck oysters and quickly sear each side with a kitchen torch, or broil each side for 30 seconds.

2. Lightly coat oysters with ginger marinade, and place on a cooling rack for 30 minutes.

3. Meanwhile, form sushi rice into 12 small, toonie-sized cakes, about ½ inch (1 cm) thick.

4. Dip bottom of each cake in sesame seeds before placing on a platter. Top each cake with wilted and well-seasoned spinach leaves. To wilt spinach, heat a small pan, add spinach, then stir gently for no more than 1 minute; season to taste.

5. Place 1 oyster on each cake, then garnish with aïoli, pickled ginger, and wasabi.

Chef's Tip: Store unused aïoli the fridge for up to 2 weeks, or cut recipe in half to avoid having any left over.

Chef's Tip: Marinade is best made 24 hours in advance and refrigerated.

Born in Quebec and trained at Montreal's Institut de tourisme et d'hôtellerie du Québec, **Chef Ronald St. Pierre** has called the Comox Valley home for more than 20 years. He has been working in partnership with local food producers to develop a sustainable local food industry. At his restaurant, Locals: Food from the Heart of the Island, his ever-changing seasonal menus and market sheets set the prevailing standard for the renowned Comox Valley food culture. The wine list has been developed to complement the diverse menu and includes select local, BC, New World, and Old World wines.

Oysters

12 fresh, medium-sized oysters

2¼ cups (560 mL) cooked sushi rice

¼ cup (60 mL) toasted sesame seeds

2 cups (500 mL) fresh spinach leaves

3 Tbsp (45 mL) pickled ginger, for garnishing

1 small stalk fresh wasabi, finely shaved, for garnishing

BBQ'd Oysters with Wasabi Cheese

Makes 4 servings

Fresh oysters, creamy cheese, and the great outdoors—now this says summer! This recipe is great because it's quick and easy, and you can adjust the recipe to make as few or as many oysters as you'd like.

1. Soak cedar plank in cold water for at least 2 hours before using.

2. Preheat the barbecue on high for 15 minutes.

3. Meanwhile, bring a pot of water to a boil and blanch asparagus for 30 seconds. Rinse under cold water to stop cooking and drain well.

4. Scrub oysters clean under cold water.

5. Pile asparagus on the cedar plank and position oysters with all the rounded ends facing the same direction, deep cup side down.

6. Place cedar plank on barbecue grill and close the lid.

7. After 2 minutes, open the lid; oysters should just be starting to open. Take out the cedar plank.

8. Remove top from each oyster and season with salt and pepper, a small pinch of ginger, and some wasabi cheese.

9. Place cedar plank back on barbecue grill and close the lid. Cook oysters for 1½ to 2 minutes longer, until cheese is melted and oysters are fully cooked.

10. Bring the whole plank to the table and enjoy each oyster with a pinch of asparagus on top.

1 cedar plank

4 oz (125 g) fresh sea asparagus (or asparagus tips)

24 Pentlatch Seafoods oysters

salt and pepper, to taste

½ tsp (2 mL) minced fresh ginger

8 oz (250 g) Natural Pastures wasabi verdelait cheese, grated (or another creamy cheese with spice, such as jalapeno)

Komo Gway Manila Clam Chowder

Chef Kathy Jerritt, Tria: Fine Catering and Gourmet Eats, Comox

Makes 10 servings

4 whole ears of corn, unshucked

3½ oz (100 g) butter

2 stalks celery, coarsely chopped

1 medium onion, coarsely chopped

½ cup (125 mL) flour

12 cups (3 L) fish stock, warm

1 cup (250 mL) dry white wine

2 cups (500 mL) whipping cream, divided

½ lb (250 g) bacon, cooked and finely chopped, plus extra for garnishing

4 medium-large potatoes, peeled, cubed, and cooked

4½ lb (2 kg) clams, shucked (see Chef's Tip)

2 lb (1 kg) clams, cooked and in the shell

dill, lightly chopped, for garnishing

Chef's Tip: Once shucked, 1 pound (500 grams) of clams produces approximately four ounces (120 grams) of meat.

Here in the Comox Valley, I usually serve this chowder in September and October, when the Komo Gway clams are prime and the corn is sweet and ripe. I make a base for the chowder first and purée it so it's silky smooth.

1. Roast corn with husks on at 450°F (220°C) for 20–25 minutes. Shuck corn and remove kernels with a sharp knife.

2. In a large pot, melt butter and lightly sweat celery and onions until they are translucent. Add flour and continue stirring mixture over medium-low heat for 5 minutes.

3. Using a whisk to combine, slowly pour warm stock into the mixture, then add white wine. Let mixture simmer on low for 20–25 minutes.

4. Remove from heat and purée. Return to heat and add 1¼ cups (310 mL) whipping cream. Keep the soup warm over low heat until needed.

5. Place a pan over medium-high heat. Add bacon and potatoes and sauté lightly until warm; add corn and shucked clams. Add remaining cream and sauté until cream thickens slightly.

6. Add cooked in-the-shell clams and mix very gently, otherwise clams will fall out.

7. Divide sauté mixture into 10 bowls and ladle hot soup over the top.

8. Garnish with more bacon and fresh dill.

Chef Kathy Jerritt resides in the beautiful Comox Valley where she owns and operates Tria: Fine Catering and Gourmet Eats. Chef Kathy believes in supporting the region's local growers and producers and bases Tria's menus on the seasonal availability of their products.

Photo: Brian Kingzett

K'omoks First Nation Big House.

Thai Green Curried Komo Gway Clams

Richard Hardy, Pentlatch Seafoods, Comox

Makes 4 servings

This fragrant curry with fresh clams is a very different take on a traditional clam recipe, and is full of the complex flavours of curry paste, coconut milk, and lemongrass.

1. Heat olive oil in a deep sauté pan over medium, and sauté garlic, lemongrass (if using), and curry paste until fragrant.

2. Add fish sauce (if using), lime juice, most of the cilantro, and coconut milk. Bring to a soft boil.

3. Add clams and steam until they open. Season with salt and pepper.

4. If you prefer extra sauce, feel free to add some chicken broth to the coconut mix. This is a matter of personal preference.

5. Garnish with freshly chopped cilantro.

1 Tbsp (15 mL) olive oil

2 cloves garlic, sliced thin

1 stalk fresh lemongrass, cut in half and bruised (optional)

2 tsp (10 mL) Thai green curry paste

1 tsp (5 mL) fish sauce (optional)

juice from 1 lime

¼ cup (60 mL) freshly chopped cilantro

11 oz (330 mL) can coconut milk

1 lb (500 g) Komo Gway clams, scrubbed

sea salt and pepper, to taste

1–2 cups (250–500 mL) chicken broth, to thin sauce (optional)

Pentlatch Seafoods Ltd. is wholly owned and sustainably operated by the K'omoks First Nation. They proudly culture Komo Gway Manila Clams and Komo Gway Pacific Oysters in the cool, clean, clear waters of Baynes Sound, British Columbia. Pentlatch Seafoods' ethos is "Honouring our Traditions—Building our Future."

Scallop, Pepper, and Pesto "Sliders"

Makes 12 pieces

12 large Qualicum Bay scallops
salt and pepper
olive oil, for searing
1 large red pepper, cut
into 12 large pieces
3 Tbsp (45 mL) basil pesto (p. 16)

Sliders are great as an appetizer or served with a side to make a full meal. And because of the red, green, and white colouring of this dish, it makes a great Christmas party addition!

1. Heat a heavy frying pan over a moderately high temperature.

2. Season scallops on both sides with salt and pepper, and add just enough oil to coat the bottom of the pan.

3. Carefully add scallops to the pan. Do not move them around. Let them sear for 1½ minutes before flipping and searing the second side for 1½ minutes.

4. If there is room in the pan, place peppers skin side down around the scallops after turning. Cook peppers for 2 minutes, skin side only.

5. Remove scallops from the pan and split in half, placing a slice of pepper between the two pieces and skewering with a cocktail stick.

6. Place a very small spoonful of pesto on top of each slider before serving.

West Coast Spot Prawn Rolls

Makes 4 servings

1 Tbsp (15 mL) honey

2 Tbsp (30 mL) soy sauce

1 clove garlic, crushed

16 large spot prawns, peeled and deveined

1 cup (250 mL) shredded Chinese cabbage

¼ cup (60 mL) shredded mustard greens

2 Tbsp (30 mL) mayonnaise (p. 8)

1 tsp (5 mL) tomato ketchup

½ tsp (2 mL) horseradish, to taste

salt and pepper, to taste

2 Tbsp (30 mL) butter

4 soft rolls

3 Tbsp (45 mL) chopped green onion, for garnishing

Think of these little rolls as high-class hot dogs. You take a bun, and then you fill it with a delicious fresh mix that is the epitome of West Coast flavours. It's that simple.

1. In a bowl, blend honey, soy sauce, and garlic, then mix in prawns; let marinate for 30 minutes.

2. Remove prawns and grill them for 2 minutes on each side, until just cooked. (Brush with more marinade as necessary.) Allow to cool slightly, then roughly chop.

3. Make the slaw by combining cabbage, mustard greens, mayonnaise, tomato ketchup, horseradish, salt, and pepper.

4. Cut and butter the rolls, then toast by grilling them lightly, cut side down.

5. Fill each roll with one-quarter of the slaw and then top with one-quarter of the chopped prawns.

6. Garnish with chopped green onion.

Queen Charlotte City on Haida Gwaii.

Mandarin Orange and Key Lime Infused Canadian Sea Salt

Andrew Shepherd, Vancouver Island Salt Company, Cobble Hill

Makes 1 lb (500 g)

2 mandarin oranges

3 key limes

1 lb (500 g) unrefined Canadian sea salt (see Chef's Tip)

Chef's Tip: If you must, you may substitute any truly unrefined sea salt, which should be a bit moist and slightly greyish.

This infused sea salt is super easy to make and tastes great with fish, fresh greens, or on the rim of your cocktail glass.

1. With a sharp fruit peeler or vegetable knife, remove skin from fruit. (Don't be too concerned if some of the white stuff is left on the skin as this will actually help the infusion.)

2. Dice fruit peel but don't overdo it as little fruit chunks are nice on the rim of your glass.

3. Thoroughly mix diced peel with sea salt, then seal mixture in a large Ziploc bag.

4. Place sealed salt in a dark cupboard and leave untouched for 24 to 36 hours.

5. When you retrieve the bag from the cupboard, the salt should be very wet and sticky with fruit juice and a bit orange in colour.

6. Dump the wet sea salt into a roasting pan and place in a preheated 250°F (120°C) oven.

7. Stir salt every 30 minutes (and more frequently if it starts to get crispy on top) until it is mostly dry. (To check readiness, pull some salt to the side so you can see the bottom of the pan; if the pan's bottom appears dry, the salt is done.)

8. Allow salt to cool thoroughly before storing in a sealed container.

Andrew Shepherd left cheffing to spend more time with his family, and decided to open his own business. As Canada's first commercial sea salt harvestry, the Vancouver Island Salt Company is filling a hole in the food scenes of Vancouver Island, BC, and Canada. VISC offers unrefined Canadian sea salt, smoked Canadian rock salts, and infused Canadian sea salts, which are all unique and are all truly Canadian.

Photo: BigTinySmalls

Free range at its finest!

Farm

The West Coast has a temperate climate with rich soils fed by rivers, and southern BC grows a wide variety of crops. These recipes celebrate the rich variety of the province's produce and have been chosen for their use of local ingredients that are readily available throughout the west.

Health-conscious and environmentally conscious growers all over the province are switching to organic methods and British Columbians are embracing the change. In addition, more and more farmers are producing organic and free-range meat that really does taste better.

Fresh

Cider Glazed Free-Range Chicken with Roasted Apples and Lemons

Makes 4 servings

4 free-range, boneless chicken breasts, skin on

salt and pepper, to taste

1 small lemon

2 medium apples, diced (and peeled, if you prefer)

¼ cup (125 mL) Sea Cider Kings & Spies cider (or any good quality dry cider)

¼ cup (125 mL) chicken stock

2 Tbsp (30 mL) oil, for frying

Chef's Tip: This dish can also be prepared with a whole roasting chicken by omitting the initial searing process and leaving the apples in large pieces.

Although you may be tempted to sample your local BC cider as you cook, make sure you save enough to flavour this succulent dish! This chicken has an amazingly tender, juicy, and fresh taste.

1. Preheat the oven to 350°F (180°C) and season chicken breasts with salt and pepper.

2. Warm an ovenproof frying pan over moderate heat and add oil, then place chicken, skin side down. Cook just this side for 8–10 minutes to render the fat and make beautiful crispy skin.

3. Meanwhile, score lemon peel with a fork to open up the essential oils, then cut into quarters.

4. When chicken skin is golden brown and crispy, turn over in the pan. Immediately add apples, cider, and lemon quarters, giving the lemons a light squeeze to release some of their juice.

5. Place pan in the preheated oven and cook for approximately 15 minutes, until the internal temperature reaches 165°F (74°C).

6. Remove pan from the oven and transfer chicken, apples, and lemons onto a platter; keep warm.

7. Place pan on high heat and add chicken stock to make a glaze by cooking over high heat until liquid has reduced down to a nice syrupy consistency.

8. Slice chicken breasts on an angle into 3 or 4 pieces, then fan out on a plate before glazing with sauce and serving with apples and lemons.

Pickled Apricots Stuffed with Blue Cheese

Makes 24 pieces

If you stuff anything with cheese, it's generally delicious. Bitter blue cheese stuffed inside sweet apricots will satisfy all your cravings and also makes a great party appetizer.

1. In a medium pot, bring water and sugar to a boil, add apricots, and cook gently for 15 minutes.
2. Add vinegar, salt, chili flakes, garlic, raisins, and onion, then cook for 5 more minutes.
3. Sterilize a 3-cup (750 mL) mason jar with boiling water for 2 minutes, then drain the boiling water out and fill with apricot mixture (including the pickling liquid).
4. Allow to cool before sealing jar. Once cooled, replace lid and store in the refrigerator until ready to use. For best results, refrigerate for at least a week before serving.
5. To serve, lift apricots out of the pickling liquid and stuff with a ball of blue cheese.

Chef's Tip: This pickling liquid may also be used to glaze baked pork or ham.

½ cup (125 mL) granulated sugar
⅔ cup (160 mL) water
24 dried apricots
⅔ cup (160 mL) rice wine vinegar
1 Tbsp (15 mL) salt
¾ tsp (4 mL) crushed chili flakes
2 cloves garlic, sliced
¼ cup (60 mL) raisins
half a small red onion, sliced
⅔ lb (350 g) soft blue cheese

Cider Braised Pork Belly with Cranberry Compote

Makes 24 pieces

Pork Belly

2 lb (1 kg) free-range pork belly

salt and pepper, to taste

2 Tbsp (30 mL) vegetable oil, for searing

1 medium onion, roughly chopped

2 cloves garlic, peeled and bruised

2½ cups (625 mL) Sea Cider Kings & Spies cider (or any good quality dry cider)

Compote

3½ oz (100 g) dried cranberries (or Craisins)

⅔ cup (160 mL) Sea Cider Kings & Spies cider (or any good quality dry cider)

half a small red onion, finely chopped

1 clove garlic, sliced

Chef's Tip: For a less tart compote, add a little brown sugar to sweeten it slightly.

This is a perfect dish to serve at parties since you can prepare it in advance and then reheat it just 10 minutes before serving. Warning: your guests won't eat just one piece!

Pork Belly

1. Warm a large pan over moderate heat.

2. Season pork belly on all sides with salt and pepper.

3. Add just enough oil to lubricate the bottom of the pan and sear all sides of pork belly until golden brown. Finish with skin side facing up.

4. Add onion and garlic to pan, placing them around the pork belly and allowing to cook for 1 minute. Add cider and bring mixture to a simmer.

5. Place pork in a small roasting pan and pour in all the liquid from the sauté pan.

6. Cook in preheated 300°F (155°C) oven for 3 hours, basting occasionally.

7. Once meat is done, remove from oven and place on a plate. Cover with another plate to weigh pork down and then refrigerate.

8. Once meat is completely cooled, remove skin from the pork belly and cut into bite-sized pieces.

9. Just before serving, warm in a 350°F (180°C) oven for 10 minutes.

Beautiful walks in the winter snow.

Compote

1. Place cranberries in a small pan with cider, red onion, and garlic.

2. Bring to a simmer over moderate heat and cook until a thick and jam-like consistency is achieved. If liquid evaporates too quickly, add additional cider or water.

3. Cool slightly, then spoon onto each pork belly just before serving.

3 Little Pigs: Chorizo Wrapped Pork Tenderloin in Smoked Bacon with Slaw

Makes 6 servings

1 medium-sized free-range
pork tenderloin
salt and pepper, to taste
2 Tbsp (30 mL) oil, for frying
8 strips smoked bacon
7 oz (200 g) chorizo sausage
6 large radishes
2 tsp (10 mL) parsley

This little piggy went into Chef Walker-Duncan's kitchen, and came out as a delicious meat lover's supper!

1. Clean tenderloin by removing any excess fat and silverskin (the sinewy white stuff on the outside), then trim the ends so tenderloin is as uniform down the entire length as possible.

2. Preheat the oven to 375°F (190°C) and warm a sauté pan over moderate-high heat.

3. Season tenderloin with salt and pepper on all sides. Add oil to the pan, swirling to coat the bottom, then sear tenderloin well on all sides, ensuring a golden brown crust is formed. Do not overcook! Remove tenderloin from pan and set aside.

4. Place a piece of plastic wrap on a work surface and lay out bacon strips so they overlap by ¹⁄₁₆ inch (2 mm), creating a sheet of bacon with one set of the ends facing you.

5. Soften sausage meat a little with your hands and spread overtop two-thirds of the bacon sheet, working from the end nearest you. Far ends of bacon should not be covered with sausage.

6. Place tenderloin on sausage meat nearest you. Use plastic wrap to lift bacon and sausage, and roll tenderloin as tightly as possible so sausage wraps all the way around it and bacon wraps right around the sausage.

Chef Steve and Claire Martin toast on the Kettle Valley Railway, above Penticton.

7. Keeping the seam at the bottom, and having removed the plastic wrap, place the bacon-wrapped chorizo tenderloin onto a roasting pan and cook for 30–40 minutes, basting occasionally.

8. Meanwhile, cut radish into very thin strips, toss with parsley, and season with just a pinch of salt and pepper.

9. Remove pork from the oven when the internal temperature reaches 160°F (60°C). Let rest for 15 minutes before slicing and serving with radish slaw.

Tomato and Mushroom Ragu

Makes 6 servings

2 Tbsp (30 mL) olive oil
¼ cup (60 mL) finely diced onion
2 garlic cloves, minced
1 cup (250 mL) sliced mushrooms
1 cup (250 mL) chopped tomatoes
salt and pepper, to taste

A great side dish you can serve alongside 3 Little Pigs!

1. In a skillet, heat oil, then sauté onion and garlic lightly. Add mushrooms and cook for 4 minutes.

2. Add tomatoes and cook for 5 minutes over high, then season with salt and pepper. Serve immediately.

Chef's Tip: Serve 3 Little Pigs (p. 100) on a plate, topped with radish slaw and Tomato and Mushroom Ragu on the side.

A classically beautiful misty morning on the beach—here at Port Renfrew.

West Coast Brussels Sauté

Makes 4 side portions or 2 lunch-sized main dishes

When *Flavours of the West Coast*'s producer was screen-testing Chef Steve, she handed him a stalk of Brussels sprouts, pointed the camera at him, and told him to "create something delicious with it whilst entertaining us." Well, he did both with style, and this is the recipe he came up with under pressure. Needless to say, it is now one of the producer's favourite lunches!

1. Cut bacon into thick strips across the layers to make "lardons" about ¼-inch (½ cm) thick.

2. Warm a skillet over moderate heat, then add the lardons and cook for 3–4 minutes, until fat has been released, but don't let them get crispy.

3. Add shallots and cook for 1 minute while stirring gently.

4. Place Brussels sprouts cut side down in the bacon fat and cook for 4–5 minutes.

5. Add butternut squash and cook for 3–4 minutes. Add ¼ cup (60 mL) water and cover pan. After 2 minutes, remove the lid and cook until excess water has evaporated and the pan is sizzling again.

6. Remove pan from heat, and let cool for a few seconds. Add cheese and stir gently so it doesn't melt completely.

7. Season with pepper and serve immediately.

4 oz (120 g) double-smoked bacon, thick sliced if possible

2 small shallots, peeled and sliced thinly

16 fresh Brussels sprouts, cut in half

1 cup (250 mL) peeled and diced butternut squash

3 oz (90 g) smoked cheddar cheese, cut into thin strips

ground black pepper, to taste

Chef's Tip: In place of bacon, pancetta makes an excellent alternative and good quality Parmigiano-Reggiano substitutes well for smoked cheddar.

Chef's Tip: This dish makes a tasty light lunch, or serve with mashed potatoes or rice pilaf for a more substantial meal.

Red Onion Jam

Executive Chef Natasha Schooten, Watermark Beachfront Resort, Osoyoos
Makes 2 quarts (2 L)

6 red onions, julienned
¾ cup (180 mL) sugar, divided
2 tsp (10 mL) salt
2 tsp (10 mL) vegetable oil
2 Tbsp (30 mL) red wine
3.5 oz (100 mL) grenadine

This may sound like a strange thing to make but it is absolutely delicious when served as a side with a charcuterie plate, or bread and cheese. It really complements them and serves as a great colour and textural contrast too.

1. In a saucepan over medium heat, cook onions with 8 Tbsp (120 mL) of the sugar, salt, and oil for 5 minutes, until opaque.
2. Add remainder of the sugar, red wine, and grenadine; reduce heat to low. Cook until syrupy, stirring frequently to avoid burning.
3. Enjoy with charcuterie, crackers, or a nice focaccia.

As a young child, **Executive Chef Natasha Schooten** would spend hours in the kitchen looking over the shoulder of her grandmother. Her grandmother's passion and respect for food ultimately became the fuel for Natasha's successful future in the culinary arts.

Following graduation from SAIT Polytechnic in Calgary, Natasha started a seven-year career with Delta Hotels and Resorts that took her on a culinary journey across Canada from Guelph, Ontario, to Kamloops, BC. Prior to starting with the Watermark Beach Resort, Natasha worked under Chef Michael Allemeier at the Mission Hill Family Estate in Kelowna. Natasha appreciates back-to-basics cooking that incorporates fresh, local ingredients. She believes that thinking globally and sourcing locally is not just politically correct, but is also personally rewarding for chefs and growers alike.

The Logpile Lodge, Smithers.

Ratatouille Torte on a Hazelnut Crust

Makes 4 servings

4 oz (125 g) ground hazelnuts

4 oz (125g) all-purpose flour

salt and pepper, to taste

½ cup (125 mL) butter,
cut into small cubes

2 large ripe tomatoes,
halved and sliced thinly

1 large zucchini, sliced thinly

1 medium eggplant, quartered
lengthwise and sliced

2 cloves garlic, sliced thinly

1 small onion, sliced thinly

1 medium red pepper,
de-seeded and sliced

2 Tbsp (30 mL) olive oil

½ cup (125 mL) goat cheese,
crumbled (optional)

First, say it out loud: *Rat-A-Too-eee*. Wasn't that fun? This vegetarian dish is delicious and packed full of protein thanks to hazelnuts that grow so well in the Fraser Valley.

1. In a large bowl, blend hazelnuts and flour with a pinch of salt and pepper.

2. Rub butter into flour mixture with your fingertips or a pastry cutter until mixture resembles coarse breadcrumbs. Add just enough cold water to form a smooth dough.

3. Wrap the dough and chill in the refrigerator for 30 minutes.

4. Divide the dough into 4 equal pieces and form into balls, then press flat, making sure the edges are solid and not split. Lay a circle of parchment paper 7 inches (18 cm) across and roll out the dough on top of it with a rolling pin into circles approximately 5 inches (13 cm) in diameter.

5. Using your thumb and forefinger, pinch the edge of each round of dough to create a crust ½ inch (2.5 mm) high.

6. Preheat the oven to 375°F (190°C).

7. Starting at the outer edge of each crust, overlap alternating vegetables in a spiral shape, working your way toward the centre until the entire pastry is covered and you have used up one-quarter of the vegetables.

Hazelnuts, at Canadian Hazelnut in the Fraser Valley.

8. Drizzle liberally with olive oil and season with salt and pepper before sliding the parchment paper onto a baking sheet.

9. Bake for 20–25 minutes until the edges are golden brown and the vegetables have begun to caramelize.

10. If desired, sprinkle with crumbled goat cheese and serve with fresh mixed greens.

Warm Spinach and Mushroom Salad with Wine Vinegar Dressing

Executive Chef Paul Cecconi, Local Lounge and Grille, Summerland

Makes 4 servings

This hearty salad eats like a meal and is full of contrasting flavours and textures. A real summer treat.

1. Blend goat cheese and whipping cream together thoroughly until smooth; set aside.

2. In a large bowl, loosely combine spinach and watercress.

3. Over medium heat, sauté shallots and garlic in olive oil until lightly golden.

4. Add mushrooms and cook for 2 minutes.

5. Add rhubarb and cook until tender. Add chicken stock to deglaze the pan.

6. Add white wine vinegar and honey, and simmer for 3–4 minutes.

7. Spoon warm dressing over salad greens to wilt the leaves slightly, then toss gently.

8. Divide dressed greens among 4 serving plates and scatter lamb bacon (with the fat) overtop. Drizzle with goat cheese dressing and serve warm.

4 oz (125 g) goat cheese
¼ cup (60 mL) whipping cream
8 cups (2 L) baby organic spinach
1 small bunch watercress
1 Tbsp (15 mL) extra virgin olive oil
1 clove garlic, chopped
2 small shallots, sliced
1 cup (250 mL) mixed mushrooms (see Chef's Note)
2–3 stalks rhubarb, thinly sliced
¼ cup (60 mL) chicken stock
2 Tbsp (30 mL) white wine vinegar
1 Tbsp (15 mL) honey
4–6 slices lamb bacon, cut into thin strips and fried until crispy

Chef's Tip: Shiitakes, morels, shimejis, and chanterelles all work well in this recipe. Instead of lamb bacon, you can also use pork bacon or pancetta. Any light fruit-infused vinegar may be substituted for the white wine vinegar.

Born and raised in North Vancouver, **Executive Chef Paul Cecconi** now works at Local Lounge and Grille in Summerland. Chef Cecconi realized his interest in food at the age of 13 and has developed his creative and fresh cooking style by working at a variety of restaurants, from a bakery to a large selection of fine dining restaurants.

Grilled Peach and Spinach Salad with Strawberry Chardonnay Vinaigrette

Makes 2 servings

Salad and Vinaigrette

1 large peach

4–6 strawberries

¾ tsp (4 mL) Dijon mustard

2 Tbsp (30 mL) Chardonnay
(or another off-dry white wine)

salt and freshly cracked pepper, to taste

⅓ cup (80 mL) vegetable oil

1 cup (250 mL) spinach
(or purslane if available)

½ cup (125 mL) candied pecans
(p. 111, or storebought)

5 oz (150 g) goat cheese

There couldn't be a tastier way to get your vitamins! Peaches may not seem like a normal item for the barbecue, but try them slightly charred in this fresh salad and they may soon replace the steaks. And if you are in the Oliver/Osoyoos region and can mix purslane in with the spinach (or use only purslane), then your vitamin and taste quotient will both skyrocket!

Salad and Vinaigrette

1. Preheat a grill pan or barbecue to high; ensure the grill/bars are very clean and very hot.

2. Cut peach in half by following the line in the skin, twist firmly to separate halves and remove the stone. Lightly oil the grill pan or barbecue and add peach halves cut side down. Cook for 6–7 minutes, until peaches are slightly charred.

3. Meanwhile, prepare the vinaigrette by placing strawberries in a medium bowl and mashing thoroughly with a fork (or use a food processor for a smoother finish), then add mustard, Chardonnay, a pinch of salt, and a generous pinch of pepper. Whisk well with the fork.

4. Slowly add oil, whisking all the time with the fork until all of it is added.

5. Wash spinach, drain well, and divide between 2 plates.

6. Slice peaches into wedges and arrange on top of the spinach, scatter candied pecans and crumbled goat cheese overtop.

7. Drizzle with strawberry vinaigrette.

Candied Pecans

1. Combine 2 cups (500 mL) water with white sugar in a large pan and bring to a boil.

2. Add pecan halves and simmer for 30 minutes.

3. Remove from heat and allow to cool for 30 minutes in the syrup.

4. Drain well and spread out on a parchment-lined baking sheet, then bake in a 325°F (170°C) oven for 20–30 minutes until pecans look "frosted."

5. Allow candied nuts to cool before storing in an airtight container and hiding them in a place where no one can find them, otherwise they won't be there when you need them!

Chef's Tip: Candied pecans make a great gift too: seal them in a jar and decorate it with a label and a bow, and you will be a very popular gift giver!

Candied Pecans

1 lb (500 g) white sugar
1 lb (500 g) pecan halves

Green Bean and Heirloom Tomato Salad with Chardonnay Vinaigrette

Executive Chef Jeremy Luypen, Terrafina at Hester Creek, Oliver

Makes 2 servings

Chardonnay Vinaigrette

5 Tbsp (75 mL) lemon juice

4 tsp (20 mL) minced fresh dill

4 tsp (20 mL) minced fresh tarragon

5 Tbsp (75 mL) Chardonnay
(or another off-dry white wine)

1 Tbsp (15 mL) Dijon mustard

5 Tbsp (75 mL) maple syrup

1⅓ cups (325 mL) grapeseed oil

salt and pepper, to taste

Salad

5 oz (150 g) green beans

2 oz (60 g) pickled red onions

4 heirloom tomatoes

2 oz (60 g) goat cheese

1 small bunch fresh pea shoots

This fresh salad is bright on the eyes and on the palette. Fresh flavours dance on your tongue with the fruity tang of Chardonnay. This is how summer would taste on a plate.

1. Mix all the vinaigrette ingredients in a blender, except for oil, salt, and pepper.

2. With blender running, slowly add oil, then season to taste.

3. Assemble salad ingredients on the plate as desired, and then drizzle vinaigrette overtop. Alternately, the ingredients may be tossed in the vinaigrette before plating, with the exception of the goat cheese and pea shoots, which are added after the salad is tossed.

Executive Chef and **Proprietor Jeremy Luypen** knew at a young age that he enjoyed cooking for friends and family. He wrote in his Grade 7 yearbook that he wanted to be a chef when he grew up! Jeremy graduated top of his class from the Culinary Arts program at Okanagan University College in Kelowna. He has cooked at the Chicago Chophouse in Calgary, was executive chef at Hotel Eldorado in the Okanagan, and is currently the executive chef at Terrafina at Hester Creek in Osoyoos, which he co-owns. Jeremy loves food and wine equally. His skills have led him to a position where he is able to use amazing local products alongside local wines to create the ultimate culinary and wine experience.

Heirloom tomatoes come in such a wonderful array of colours.

Organic Beetroot Salad with Creamy Cheese

Executive Winery Chef Matthew Batey, Mission Hill Family Estate, Kelowna

Makes 4 servings

16 small beets, greens removed

balsamic vinegar

1 piece star anise

1 cinnamon stick

½ tsp (2 mL) fresh thyme

good quality olive oil, to taste

salt, to taste

12 mint leaves, torn

½ cup (125 mL) blackberries

4 oz (130 g) The Farm House Lady Jane goat cheese (or other creamy cheese)

At the core of this dish are fantastic locally grown and produced ingredients. It seems obvious but there isn't a substitute for in-season, locally raised products. These ingredients are prepared simply yet are packed full of flavour and will pair perfectly with Mission Hill Reserve Pinot Noir.

1. After washing beets, place in a pan and just cover with a mixture of 15% balsamic vinegar and 85% water. Add star anise, cinnamon stick, and thyme. Cover pan and bring to a slow boil, then cook over medium heat until tender (approximately 30–40 minutes).

2. Once cooked, remove beets from liquid and peel while still hot, leaving stems intact. Let stand to cool.

3. Once cool, plate beets and drizzle with olive oil and salt to taste.

4. Add mint leaves and blackberries to the plate, arranged in your own artistic fashion.

5. Portion cheese as desired (1 large chunk, or several smaller chunks) and add to the plate.

6. Serve with thin crackers. Find that glass of Pinot Noir you had in your hand and enjoy.

Since arriving in the Okanagan Valley in 2007 following a distinguished restaurant cooking career, **Executive Winery Chef Matthew Batey**, Certified Chef de Cuisine, has been instrumental in forging and defining the concept of "Cuisine du Terrior"—wine country cooking with the freshest, locally grown, in-season ingredients.

As executive winery chef at Mission Hill Family Estate, Chef Batey oversees the winery's entire culinary program, including mentorship for the brigade at the Terrace Restaurant, hosting fine dining events, off-site functions, and designing the curriculum for the winery's culinary education program. In his first two years at Mission Hill, Chef Batey's efforts and creativity were recognized internationally when *Travel + Leisure Magazine* chose the Terrace Restaurant as one of the top 5 winery restaurants in the world. He proudly leads the winery's membership in the esteemed international gastronomic society Chaîne des Rôtisseurs, whose origins date back to 1248.

Beet Hummous

Carolyn Herriot, Author of *The Zero-Mile Diet*

Makes 2 cups (500 mL)

4 large beets, peeled and halved
1 cup (250 mL) cooked chickpeas
2 Tbsp (30 mL) tahini
2 garlic cloves, chopped
1 Tbsp (15 mL) ground cumin
juice of 2 lemons
1 tsp (2 mL) sea salt
freshly ground pepper, to taste

This is a colourful and tasty combination. The beets, chickpeas, and garlic can be harvested from the garden for an eye-catching topping on cucumber rounds or crackers; or just scoop some up on vegetable sticks made from carrots, peppers, and celery.

1. Cover beets with water in a saucepan and simmer for about 40 minutes, testing with a knife for tenderness.
2. Place cooked beets and all the other ingredients in a food processor and pulse for approximately 5–8 minutes, or until smooth.
3. Taste and adjust seasonings as desired.
4. Chill before serving, and keep refrigerated.

Carolyn Herriot discovered it takes only five years to become self-sufficient in fruits and vegetables year-round, so she wrote *The Zero-Mile Diet*, which follows her year of organic homegrown food production, and saving seeds for future harvests. This is a recipe from her next book, *The Zero-Mile Diet Cookbook*, which is a delicious way to eat healthy by connecting the garden harvest to the kitchen.

Cider Pumpkin Soup

Makes 6–8 servings

4 or 5 lb (1.8–2.2 kg) pumpkin

olive oil, for roasting pumpkin

2 cloves garlic, lightly smashed

½ tsp (2 mL) dried thyme
(or use 3 sprigs fresh thyme)

salt and pepper

1 Tbsp (15 mL) olive oil

2 tsp (10 mL) fresh ginger, grated

½ cup (125 mL) peeled,
cored, and chopped apple

½ cup (125 mL) chopped onion

¼ cup (60 mL) chopped carrot

¼ cup (60 mL) chopped celery

1 tsp (5 mL) salt

½ tsp (2 mL) pepper

3 cups (750 mL) dry cider

½ cup (125 mL) whipping
cream, for garnishing

Apple Garnish (optional; p. 119)

Never feel guilty about wasting pumpkin flesh at Halloween again; this delicious soup will soon be an eagerly anticipated part of your Halloween traditions.

1. Cut pumpkin in half through the middle and scoop out the seeds (reserve for the garnish). Rub inside of pumpkin with olive oil, garlic, thyme, salt, and pepper.

2. Place pumpkin on a baking sheet and roast in a 350°F (175°C) oven for 45 minutes, until soft and tender.

3. Allow pumpkin to cool and remove garlic and thyme. Using a large spoon, scrape out the flesh and reserve it. Discard the skin.

4. In a large heavy pan, warm olive oil over medium heat, and then add ginger, apple, onion, carrot, and celery. Season with salt and pepper and cook for 10 minutes, stirring frequently. Do not allow vegetables to colour.

5. Add reserved pumpkin flesh, cook for 4–5 minutes, and then add cider. Bring to a gentle simmer for 20 minutes.

6. Purée the mixture in a food processor, or use an electric hand blender. (For a very smooth finish, press liquid through a fine-meshed sieve using a ladle.)

7. Reheat the soup and drizzle whipping cream overtop as a garnish. If desired, serve with toasted pumpkin seeds and apple slices.

Apple Garnish

1. Quarter an apple, then slice each quarter into 3–4 slices. Mix well with honey, lemon juice, and a pinch of cinnamon and nutmeg.

2. Place apple slices on a parchment-lined baking sheet. Bake for 20 minutes at 325°F (160°C).

3. Wash pumpkin seeds under cold water in a fine-meshed sieve, then dry on a paper towel. Mix with a pinch of salt, cayenne pepper, brown sugar, and paprika.

4. Spread spiced seeds on a parchment-lined baking sheet and roast in a 350°F (180°C) oven for 10–12 minutes, or until lightly golden brown.

5. Cool slices and seeds and store in an airtight container for up to 1 week. Use to garnish cider pumpkin soup.

Apple Garnish

1 whole apple
1 tsp (5 mL) honey
1 tsp (5 mL) lemon juice
cinnamon
nutmeg
pumpkin seeds saved from a small pumpkin
salt
cayenne pepper
brown sugar
paprika

Port Hardy.

Mission Hill Winery, Kelowna.

Bannock

Makes 1 loaf

"Bannock" refers to a variety of flat bread that was the staple of early gold rush pioneers. They could easily make it on the trail because it doesn't need yeast and can be cooked over a campfire. It's still just as easy and delicious today; try making it on your next camping expedition!

3 cups (750 mL) all-purpose flour
1 tsp (5 mL) salt
2 Tbsp (30 mL) baking powder
¼ cup (60 mL) melted butter

1. In a large bowl, combine flour, salt, and baking powder.
2. Pour melted butter and 1½ cups (375 mL) water overtop, then stir with a fork to form a ball.
3. Turn onto a lightly floured surface, and knead gently into a smooth dough.
4. Shape dough into a flat loaf about 1 inch (2.5 cm) thick.
5. Place in a heavy, greased frying pan (cast iron is ideal) and cook over medium-low heat for about 15 minutes on each side.

Chef's Tip: Bannock may also be baked on a greased or parchment-lined baking sheet at 350°F (175°C) for 25–30 minutes.

Focaccia Bread

Nick Versteeg, Co-Producer, *The Next Great Chef*

Makes 1 large loaf

Starter Dough

1⅔ cups (400 mL) water at 70°F
(21°C) (see Chef's Tip)

½ tsp (2 mL) instant yeast

2½ cups (625 mL) bread flour

Focaccia Dough

5 cups (1.25 L) bread flour

2 cups (500 mL) water at 104°F (35°C)
(see Chef's Tip)

2 Tbsp (30 mL) instant yeast

1 Tbsp (15 mL) salt

starter dough

Suggested Toppings

caramelized onions

roasted red peppers

artichoke hearts (cut)

olives (sliced)

fresh herbs - rosemary,
thyme, or oregano

grated cheese - Parmesan,
Asiago, or goat

Oven-fresh bread is great on its own, but throw in some extra flavour with herbs, red peppers, and artichokes, and you have yourself an amazing taste. The more herbs you add, the more flavour you'll enjoy, or you can keep it simple–as you prefer.

Starter Dough

1. In a large bowl, combine water and yeast, stirring until yeast is completely dissolved.

2. Add bread flour and blend until a smooth consistency is reached.

3. Cover with a lid or plastic wrap so no crust can form.

4. Allow to ferment at room temperature for 16–18 hours.

Chef's Tip: The recipe calls for 1⅔ cups (400 mL) water, but that is only an approximate amount; use enough to create a thick batter-like consistency.

Focaccia Dough

1. Place flour, water, yeast, salt, and starter dough into a stand mixer with a dough hook (see Chef's Tip if mixing by hand).

2. Mix on low for 6 minutes, periodically scraping the bottom of the bowl to ensure uniform mixing. Mix on medium speed for 3–4 minutes.

3. Place dough in an oiled container, making sure the dough's internal temperature is 75°F (24°C). If not, place in a warm environment until desired temperature is achieved.

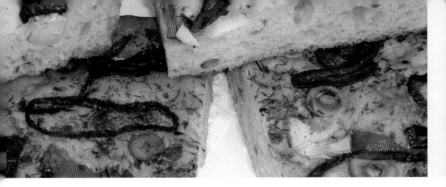

4. In an ideal situation, give the dough one "stretch and fold" every 30 minutes. In total, give the dough 3 stretch and folds over 2 hours. The total time of bulk fermentation should not exceed 2¼ hours.

5. Spread out dough on an olive oiled sheet pan. Don't force the dough: use your fingers to lightly punch it so that it's even, pausing very briefly every few seconds.

6. Allow dough to rise for 20 minutes in a warm place, then push dough to outside of sheet pan with fingers, and allow to proof for 45–60 minutes. Add your choice of toppings (see Chef's Tip).

7. Bake for a minimum of 20–25 minutes at 450°F (240°C) in a convection oven. If you don't have a convection oven, make sure to increase the temperature by 25 degrees.

Chef's Tip: When preparing the dough, the water temperature should be about 100–104°F (33–35°C), which will feel warm to the touch but not hot.

Chef's Tip: If mixing and kneading by hand, bring all the ingredients together and knead for 6–8 minutes on a lightly floured surface until a smooth, elastic consistency is achieved.

Chef's Tip: If you are adding cheese as one of your toppings, add the cheese after three-quarters of the baking time has elapsed.

For the past 30 years, **Nick Versteeg** has been producing and directing culinary shows and documentaries for television, including a variety of specials for the US and Canadian Food Networks, and has won several awards. Among other projects, he has co-produced two seasons of *The Next Great Chef* and has produced two celebrated documentaries on food security and food sustainability: *Island on the Edge* (2008) and *Food Security, it's in your hands* (2011). Nick lives in the Cowichan Valley on Vancouver Island, where he loves baking with local grains in his wood-fired oven.

Heirloom Tomato and Pickle Bruschetta

Makes 4 servings

Bruschetta is a dish that's simple to make but that is sure to impress company. This bruschetta mixture can be prepared the day before and kept in the fridge.

1. Preheat the oven to 350°F (180°C).
2. Cut baguette slices on a 45-degree angle as thick as desired, place on a baking sheet, and bake for 6–8 minutes, until just lightly golden brown.
3. When cool enough to handle, rub slices gently with garlic clove and top with a wedge of cheese.
4. In a small bowl, combine tomatoes, onion, pickles, olive oil, salt, and pepper; mix gently.
5. Top bread and cheese slices with spoonfuls of tomato mixture, then drizzle with balsamic vinegar. Finish with a sprinkle of sea salt.

1 thin baguette

1 clove garlic, peeled

1 small round Camembert or brie-style cheese, cut into thin wedges

20 heirloom cherry tomatoes, quartered

1 small onion, finely diced

3 Tbsp (45 mL) thinly sliced sweet pickles

3 Tbsp (45 mL) olive oil

1 tsp (5 mL) coarse sea salt

1 tsp (5 mL) freshly cracked pepper

2 Tbsp (30 mL) balsamic vinegar

City

Scene through a glass.

Like music, food styles are always changing, and many of them don't fall under traditional categories anymore. Modern-day Canada is an amalgam of cultures from all over the world, each contributing its own unique cuisine and flavours. This is reflected in the exciting new foods emerging in our cities where "fusion" is the buzzword, from the very best restaurants to the vendors on the street. This process has been going on for the last 150 years, from the importing of coconuts used by the gold rush miners in Barkerville to the exotic spices epitomized by Vij's Restaurant in Vancouver. Food in our cities is vibrant, new, and, above all, exciting. Combine that with a renewed awareness of fresh and organic produce and it's a great time to eat in the city!

Cuisine

Wor Wonton Soup with Chicken, Shrimp, Crab, and Organic Vegetables

Makes 4 servings

4 cups (1 L) well-flavoured chicken stock (add more base to make it stronger in flavour)

4 cups (1 L) light chicken stock (see Chef's Tip)

5 oz (160 g) white chicken meat or pork

2 Tbsp (30 mL) whipping cream

1 Tbsp (15 mL) soy sauce

salt and pepper, to taste

16 wonton wrappers

2½ oz (75 g) peeled shrimp

2½ oz (75 g) crabmeat

1 cup (250 mL) broccoli florets, cooked quickly in light chicken stock

½ cup (60 mL) thinly sliced carrots, cooked quickly in light chicken stock

½ cup (60 mL) thinly sliced red peppers

This is one of those recipes where you can use leftovers to make a delicious meal, and no one will know. Use whatever ingredients you like best!

1. In two separate pans, bring chicken stocks to a gentle simmer.

2. Place chicken and whipping cream in a food processor with soy sauce and a pinch of salt and pepper. Pulse lightly to blend well but do not make into a paste. Divide into 16 portions.

3. Wet the edge of half of a wonton wrapper with water and add a portion of chicken mix to the middle. Fold wrapper in half, pinching the seal with your fingers from one side to the other. This will expel any air and form a tight seal. Repeat with other wonton wrappers.

4. Drop wontons a few at a time into the light stock and cook for 3–4 minutes. Drain and set aside.

5. Divide wontons, shrimp, crabmeat, broccoli, carrots, and red peppers among 4 large bowls, then pour hot strong chicken stock overtop. Serve immediately.

Chef's Tip: To make light chicken stock, combine equal parts water and regular chicken stock.

Totem pole in the Royal BC Museum gardens in Victoria.

Floral Summer Roll with Curried Pork Belly

Chef Tobias MacDonald, La Belle Auberge

Makes 6 servings

Pork Filling

¾ cup plus 1 Tbsp (200 mL)
chicken stock

1 stalk lemongrass, finely chopped

½ inch (1 cm) knob
ginger, finely chopped

12 oz (330 mL) can coconut milk

1 tsp (5 mL) red curry paste

3½ Tbsp (50 mL) fish sauce

1 cup (250 mL) peeled
and cubed butternut squash

10 oz (300 g) pork belly, cooked
and cut into ½-inch (1 cm) cubes

3 shiitake mushrooms,
sliced and blanched

salt and pepper, to taste

1 Tbsp (15 mL) lemon juice (optional)

Floral Summer Roll

24 rice paper sheets, 8-inch (20 cm)
squares or rounds

1 bunch edible flowers (optional)

1 head radicchio, chiffonaded
(see Chef's Tip, p. 31)

1 shiitake mushroom,
sliced and blanched

1 bunch cilantro

1 lime, segmented (optional)

2 oz (60 g) crushed peanuts (optional)

It can't be a bad thing to have a little choice, can it? You can replace most of the fresh ingredients in this stunning dish with other ingredients that you love—as long as they're beautiful and delicious, of course! The build-it-yourself component makes this hands-on dish fun to make and to eat.

Pork Filling

1. Over medium heat, bring chicken stock to a simmer with lemongrass and ginger. Simmer for 30 minutes, then add coconut milk, curry paste, and fish sauce.

2. Strain soup through a fine sieve and discard the pulp. Return broth to the pot and add squash. Cook until squash is soft.

3. Add the sauce to the pork belly and shiitakes and mix. Season to taste with salt, pepper, and a squeeze of lemon juice.

4. Keep pork mixture warm in the saucepan while you prepare the floral summer rolls.

Floral Summer Roll

1. In a bowl, soak rice paper sheet in hot water for 30 seconds, or until pliable. Place rice paper on an oiled piece of plastic wrap and sprinkle with a portion of edible flowers, radicchio, shiitake, and a few sprigs of cilantro. Top with a second sheet of rice paper to make a floral "sandwich."

2. Cover with another sheet of oiled plastic wrap and cut into a square, then remove plastic wrap from both sides of the sandwich. Prepare remaining wrappers the same way.

3. Lay out rice paper wrappers on a plate. Spoon warm pork filling into a small bowl and present it on the side of the plate.

4. These summer rolls are "build it yourself," so serve with crushed peanuts, segmented lime wedges, or any other garnish you like.

Tobias MacDonald grew up in Crawford Bay, BC. His restaurant career began at a local golf course the old-fashioned way: washing dishes and then cooking as a way to pay his way through school. It was here he developed his passion for cooking. In Vancouver, he worked for a period at Scott Jaeger's Pear Tree, before taking an apprenticeship under Bruno Marti at La Belle Auberge Restaurant in Ladner. He then moved abroad to Switzerland to work at Schloss Falkenstein with Max Eichmann. Returning to Vancouver, Tobias went back to La Belle Auberge as chef de cuisine.

In 2005, he joined Culinary Team Canada to compete in Basle at the Salon Culinaire Mondial, where the team received two gold medals and 1st place in the hot kitchen. In 2006, the team competed in Expogast in Luxembourg, where they won three gold medals and 4th overall. Tobias became the captain of the team and went on to garner three gold medals and one silver at the American Culinary Classic in Chicago for a 2nd place finish.

Tobias loves working with local farmers to get the freshest seasonal produce available in Ladner and is constantly looking to evolve his cooking style.

West Coast Sushi

Makes 4 servings

2 cups (500 mL) sushi rice

⅔ cup (180 mL) rice wine vinegar

½ cup (125 mL) sugar

4 tsp (20 mL) salt

5 oz (150 g) chanterelle mushrooms,
fresh or rehydrated

2 Tbsp (30 mL) vegetable oil

salt and white pepper, to taste

5 oz (150 g) sushi grade salmon

4 oz (120 g) cooked
clams, finely chopped

8 nori seaweed sheets

pickled ginger, for garnishing

wasabi paste, for dipping

soy sauce, for dipping

This is the perfect meal for people who like to play with their food. You can decide to roll the sushi with clams and salmon, or take a vegetarian approach and use chanterelle mushrooms instead. Either way, they're delicious!

1. Rinse rice under cold water quickly to remove excess starch.

2. In the top of a double boiler, bring 2½ cups (625 mL) water to a boil. Add rice and return to a boil, then cover tightly and place over hot water for 20 minutes only. You can also use a rice cooker if you don't have a double boiler; adjust cooking time accordingly.

3. Remove lid and gently fluff rice to ensure it is cooked. If it requires more cooking, re-cover and allow to finish cooking for 5–10 minutes more.

4. Meanwhile, place vinegar, sugar, and salt in a small pot and bring to a rapid boil for 1 minute. Allow to cool.

5. Tip rice into a large bowl or shallow tray and spread out very gently with a spatula or baking scraper. Drizzle one-third of the vinegar mixture evenly over rice and lightly toss rice to coat evenly. Repeat twice more, allowing rice to cool a little between each addition.

6. Split chanterelles into long, thin strips.

7. Warm a frying pan over moderate heat, add oil, and gently cook chanterelles until wilted and tender. Season with salt and pepper.

8. Slice salmon into long, thin strips, and season lightly with salt and white pepper.

9. Lay a nori sheet on a sushi rolling mat and cover the closest three-quarters of it with one-eighth of rice mixture. Spread out evenly and then lay one-quarter of the chanterelles in a line along the bottom. Roll into a tight log using the mat for shaping.

10. Repeat using salmon and clams as filling, laying salmon strips lengthwise and spreading clam meat over bottom one-third of nori sheet before rolling.

11. Slice rolls into 1-inch (2.5 cm) slices and serve with pickled ginger, soy sauce, and wasabi.

CBC's Gloria Macarenko rolls sushi in the *Flavours* studio kitchen.

Vikram's Goat Curry

From *Vij's at Home: Relax, Honey* by Meeru Dhalwala & Vikram Vij

Makes about 8 servings

Stewed Goat

½ cup (125 mL) ghee or butter

1 tsp (5 mL) salt

6 lb (2.7 kg) goat meat, bone in, cut into 1½–2-inch (4–5 cm) cubes (substitute beef if desired)

Masala

½ cup (125 mL) cooking oil

1 Tbsp plus 1 tsp (20 mL) cumin seeds

10 whole cloves

3-inch (8 cm) cinnamon stick

5 black cardamom pods, lightly pounded (optional)

1 large red onion, thinly sliced

9 medium cloves garlic, chopped

2 Tbsp (30 mL) finely chopped ginger

3 cups (750 mL) puréed tomatoes, fresh or canned

1 tsp (5 mL) black pepper

2 Tbsp (30 mL) ground cumin

2 Tbsp (30 mL) garam masala

1 tsp (5 mL) turmeric

1½ tsp (7.5 mL) salt

1 Tbsp (30 mL) paprika (optional)

1½ tsp (7.5 mL) cayenne pepper (optional)

1 cup (250 mL) plain yogourt (minimum 2% milk fat), stirred

The prep and cooking time for this curry is 2½ hours. Vikram loves to spend a Sunday afternoon luxuriously chopping, mixing, and getting just about every dish and spoon in the kitchen dirty. This curry is definitely worth the mess! Serve with white or brown basmati rice or naan.

Stewed Goat

1. In a large pot over medium-high heat, combine ghee (or butter), salt, goat meat, and 1 cup (250 mL) water. Stir regularly for 10–15 minutes, or until meat is browned and begins to release its juices.

2. Cover and reduce heat to low, then cook for 75 minutes, stirring every 15 minutes. The goat meat and bones will release water and should not stick to the bottom of the pan. If meat is sticking, add ½ to 1 cup (125–250 mL) more water. While goat meat is stewing, make the masala in a separate pan.

Masala

1. In a large pot, heat oil over medium-high for 1 minute. Add cumin seeds, cloves, cinnamon, and cardamom pods; stir and allow cumin seeds to sizzle for 30 seconds. Stir in onion and sauté for 7 to 8 minutes, or until crispy brown at the edges.

2. Add garlic and sauté for 2 minutes, or until browned. Stir in ginger, tomatoes, black pepper, ground cumin, garam masala, turmeric, salt, paprika, and cayenne. Reduce heat to medium, cover, and cook for 3 minutes.

3. Place yogourt in a small bowl. To prevent curdling, spoon 2 to 3 Tbsp (30–45 mL) of the hot masala into the yogourt. Stir well, and then pour the yogourt mixture into the pot of masala. Sauté masala for another 2 minutes, then stir in 6 cups (1.5 L) water.

4. Increase heat to high and bring to a boil. Cover, reduce heat to low, and simmer for 10 minutes. Turn off the heat.

5. After goat has stewed for 75 minutes, remove a piece from the pot, allow it to cool for a minute, and pull some meat off the bone. If it pulls off easily and is tender, remove the pot from the heat. If not, cook goat meat for another 15 minutes.

6. Once goat meat is cooked, turn off the heat, and allow it to cool for 20 to 30 minutes.

7. Set the pot of cooled goat meat beside the pot of curry. Wearing plastic gloves, pull the goat meat off the bones. Discard the bones and return the goat meat to the pot of curry.

8. Just before serving, heat goat curry over medium-high and bring to a boil. Stir and reduce heat to medium, cover, and simmer for 10 minutes. Serve immediately.

Vikram Vij was born in India in 1964, and lived in New Delhi and Bombay until 1984. He studied hotel management in Austria and worked and lived in Salzburg and Vienna until 1989, when he moved to Canada to work at the Banff Springs Hotel. In September 1994, Vikram opened Vij's Restaurant in Vancouver, BC, and his wife, Meeru, joined him a year later. In 2002, Vikram and Meeru opened up a second restaurant and market called Rangoli.

Vikram is past president and an active member of the Chef's Table Society of British Columbia, which is dedicated to supporting innovative and sustainable food programs involving chefs, producers, and others working in the local food industry. Vikram is not only a chef but also a certified sommelier.

Toad in the Hole

Makes 4 servings

1 ½ cups (375 mL) milk

2 eggs

¾ cup (185 mL) all-purpose flour

salt and pepper, to taste

1 ½ lb (750 g) chorizo sausages
(or less spicy sausages if preferred)

Onion Gravy

2 Tbsp (30 mL) oil (or
use excess chorizo fat)

1 lb (500 g) red onion, sliced

2 Tbsp (30 mL) all-purpose flour

2 cups (500 mL) beef stock, warm

salt and pepper, to taste

Amphibian lovers be reassured, no actual toads were harmed in the making of this product. Toad in the Hole is a British classic of sausages in a Yorkshire pudding batter.

1. In a small bowl, whisk milk and eggs together well.

2. In a large bowl, blend together flour with salt and pepper, then make a well in the middle.

3. Pour egg and milk into the well and whisk together lightly. Do not overmix; a few little lumps are fine. Allow to rest at room temperature for at least 30 minutes.

4. Preheat the oven to 400°F (200°C).

5. Place sausages in an ovenproof dish and cook in the oven for 15 minutes.

6. Add a little splash of hot water to the batter, then whisk lightly to break up any remaining lumps.

7. Remove the sausages from the oven and, working as quickly as possible, drain any excess oil from the baking dish, arrange the sausages evenly, and pour the batter overtop. Return to the oven for 30 minutes.

8. Place a heavy pan on the stove and warm over moderate heat for the onion gravy. Add oil and onions, cooking until onions are golden brown, sprinkling flour overtop and stirring well to absorb the fat. If it looks oily, a little more flour may be added.

9. Add the stock in 3 stages, stirring well after each addition and making sure there are no lumps before adding additional stock; bring the liquid to a full boil. Reduce the heat and simmer for 10 minutes. Season with salt and pepper.

10. Toad in the Hole should be well risen and nicely browned. Cut into serving portions and serve with onion gravy overtop.

Southwestern Meatloaf

Chef John Cantin, John's Place, Victoria

Makes 1 loaf

Meatloaf

2 lb (1 kg) medium ground beef

⅔ lb (350 g) ground pork

2 cups (500 mL) crumbled cornbread

1 whole medium white onion, finely chopped and sautéed in vegetable oil

2 cloves fresh garlic, chopped

½ cup (125 mL) salsa

5 eggs

1 Tbsp (15 mL) black pepper

1 Tbsp (15 mL) salt

half a bunch chopped fresh cilantro

Marsala Sauce

1 Tbsp (15 mL) butter

6 fresh white mushrooms, sliced

quarter of a medium onion, chopped finely

4 Tbsp (60 mL) Italian Marsala wine

½ cup (125 mL) whipping cream

1 cup (250 mL) prepared demi-glace gravy (see Chef's Tip)

salt and pepper, to taste

Meatloaf is the epitome of comfort food. This recipe makes an amazing dinner, and there may even be leftovers for sandwiches the next day!

Meatloaf

1. In a large bowl, mix all the ingredients by hand.
2. Shape into a long tube or use a bread pan and mould to the shape of the pan.
3. Wrap in aluminum foil, twirling the ends like a cigar.
4. Place on a tray and cook at 350°F (180°C) for 50 minutes.

Marsala Sauce

1. Over medium heat, sauté butter, mushrooms, and onion for 4–5 minutes.
2. Add Marsala wine and whipping cream, let reduce for 2–3 minutes, and then add demi-glace gravy.
3. Reduce until thick, and then add black pepper and salt.
4. Pour overtop meatloaf before serving.

Chef's Tip: If you don't want to prepare demi-glace from scratch, packaged Knorr Demi-glace is a great substitute.

John's Place has been an icon in downtown Victoria since 1984.

Born in Windsor, Ontario, **Chef John Cantin** attended culinary school at St. Clair College. John completed his apprenticeship in Europe and Israel and was a junior member of Team Canada at the Culinary Olympics in Frankfurt in 1976. John also won a gold medal in Jerusalem in 1978. John has been the proud chef-owner of John's Place Restaurant in Victoria, BC, since 1984. John's homemade, fresh comfort food has gathered a lot of attention around Canada, and he has been featured on Food Network Canada and numerous local TV shows.

The producer was distracted during the filming at Port Edward by this gorgeous bank of wild foxgloves. Everything had to stop for a moment while we took in the beauty of them.

Cataplana

Richard Hardy, Pentlatch Seafoods, and Chef Kathy Jerritt, Tria: Fine Catering and Gourmet Eats

Makes 6 servings

Cataplana is a wonderful Portuguese dish combining pork and clams. Cataplana is the name for both the recipe and the vessel in which you cook it. The traditional dish is made of copper and shaped like two clamshells hinged at one end. Don't worry if you don't have a spare cataplana among your kitchen cooking equipment; any pot with a lid will do! We used Pentlatch Seafoods' Komo Gway clams and Tannadice Farms pork belly in this dish.

2 Tbsp (30 mL) grapeseed oil (or other fine vegetable oil)

1 lb (500 g) pork belly or pork butt, cut into 2-inch (5 cm) pieces

salt and pepper, to taste

¾ cup (185 mL) white wine, divided

¼ cup (60 mL) olive oil

3 medium onions, julienned

3 cloves garlic, crushed

1 tsp (5 mL) smoked paprika

1 bay leaf

1 lb (500 g) tomatoes, peeled (canned is fine)

¼ lb (125 g) sliced chorizo (dry-cured variety, not fresh)

3 lb (1.5 kg) clams in the shell

springs of fresh parsley, coarsely chopped, for garnishing

1. Add grapeseed oil to a large pot over medium-high heat. Season pork with salt and pepper, then sear pork pieces on all sides. Remove from the pot and set aside. Deglaze the pan with a little bit of white wine, but be sure to reserve the deglazing liquid.

2. In the same large pot, over medium-low heat, sweat the onions and garlic in olive oil. Add smoked paprika and cook for 1 minute. Add remaining white wine, reserved deglazing wine, bay leaf, tomatoes, and pork (with all its juices).

3. Cover the pot with a lid and cook over very low heat for 2 hours.

4. After 2 hours, add chorizo and clams to the stew, then re-cover and steam until clams open up.

5. Garnish with fresh parsley.

6. Serve in the cooking vessel at the table, only uncovering the lid once everyone is seated.

Bacon, Blue Cheese, and Squash Ravioli with Apricot Vinaigrette

Makes 6 servings

Pasta Dough

1 lb (500 g) bread flour

5 eggs, beaten

1 Tbsp (15 mL) olive oil

Filling

1 cup (250 mL) roasted butternut squash, puréed (or substitute pumpkin)

1 tsp (5 mL) ground nutmeg

salt and pepper, to taste

2 cloves roasted garlic

4 strips double-smoked bacon, lightly cooked and finely chopped

2 oz (60 g) blue cheese

1 egg, beaten, for egg wash

Vinaigrette

3 Tbsp (45 mL) Vinegar Works apricot vinegar (or other fruit-flavoured vinegar)

1 tsp (5 mL) Dijon mustard

2 tsp (10 mL) chili flakes

salt and pepper, to taste

½ cup (125 mL) canola oil

2 cups (500 mL) fresh micro salad greens, for serving

shaved Parmesan to taste, for garnishing

fresh cracked pepper, for garnishing

Making pasta from scratch involves a lot of steps, but it's easier than it looks, and fresh pasta dough tastes so much better than the packaged product. If you don't have access to Vinegar Works vinegar, try another fruit-infused vinegar.

1. Place flour in a large bowl and make a well in the centre, then add eggs and oil. Mix thoroughly to form a soft but firm dough; if it's too dry, add a little water. Knead for 3–4 minutes and then let rest for 20 minutes.

2. Meanwhile, prepare vinaigrette by mixing vinegar, mustard, chili flakes, salt, and pepper in a bowl, then whisk vigorously while slowly adding oil. Set aside.

3. Mix squash purée with nutmeg, salt, pepper, and garlic.

4. Roll pasta dough out until ¹⁄₁₆ inch (2 mm) thick, then cut out 12 3½-inch (9 cm) circles.

5. Place circles on a floured surface and spoon 2 tablespoons (30 mL) squash purée into the centre of half of the circles, topped with one-sixth of the bacon and a piece of blue cheese.

6. Brush edges of each round lightly with beaten egg and place a second pasta disc overtop each one. Working around the edges, seal each ravioli carefully, expelling as much air as possible without getting any of the filling between the sealed edges.

Chef Steve and Major James Pierotti from CFB Esquimalt have fun making pasta!

7. Bring a large pot of water to a boil and cook raviolis until they float. Carefully remove pasta from water and place one into each serving dish.

8. Whisk prepared vinaigrette and use a little to dress micro salad greens before pouring the rest over raviolis.

9. Top each ravioli with a ball of microgreens and serve with shaved Parmesan and fresh black pepper.

Moroccan Spiced Vegan
Rissoles with Rhubarb Gravy

Makes 6 servings

Rissoles

3 Tbsp (45 mL) vegetable oil

1 large onion, sliced

4 cloves garlic, minced

2 Tbsp (30 mL) fresh ginger, minced

1 Tbsp (15 mL) curry powder

1 Tbsp (15 mL) ground cumin

1 Tbsp (15 mL) paprika

1 Tbsp (15 mL) tomato paste

14 oz (398 mL) can chickpeas, liquid reserved (see Chef's Tip)

1 cup (250 mL) roasted and mashed parsnip

1 cup (250 mL) toasted and skinned hazelnuts

1 cup (250 mL) cooked mung beans and brown or green lentils (if using dried, see Chef's Tip)

½ cup (125 mL) raisins (or currants), soaked in hot water for 30 minutes

salt and pepper, to taste

½ cup (125 mL) chana (chickpea flour)

I can't believe it's not meat! Chef Steve created this recipe for a vegan wedding in the Cowichan Valley, and all the guests raved about it, demanding to have the recipe. Here it is!

Rissoles

1. In a large pot over moderate heat, warm oil and then add onion, garlic, and ginger. Cook until golden brown and just beginning to stick to the bottom.

2. Add curry powder, cumin, and paprika, then cook for 3–4 minutes before adding tomato paste. Cook for another 1–2 minutes, stirring constantly.

3. Add chickpeas with the liquid from the can, stirring vigorously to scrape the bottom of the pot so it's clean. Cook until most of the liquid has evaporated.

4. Take the pot off the heat and gently stir in mashed parsnip, hazelnuts, mung beans, lentils, and raisins.

5. Check seasoning and adjust if necessary with salt and pepper. Gently stir in the chana to form a dough-like consistency, adding more chana as required.

6. Using an ice cream scoop, or a large spoon, place balls of the mixture on a parchment-lined baking sheet and cook in a 350°F (175°C) oven for 20–25 minutes. (Mixture may also be cooked in a loaf pan for 50–60 minutes.)

Rhubarb Gravy

1. In a covered pot, sweat onion in a splash of water until well cooked.

2. Add remaining ingredients and cook over moderate heat until rhubarb is soft and broken down.

3. Strain through a fine-meshed sieve and check the seasoning; more honey may be required to balance out the rhubarb's acidity. There should be a slight tartness to the gravy, not too sweet.

4. Pour gravy overtop Moroccan rissoles or serve on the side, if you prefer.

Rhubarb Gravy

1 small onion, finely chopped

3 large stalks rhubarb, roughly chopped

1 small red pepper, finely chopped

2 Tbsp (30 mL) honey

1 tsp (5 mL) caraway seeds

Chef's Tip: If using home-cooked chickpeas, they are finished when they have been boiled until tender. Reserve the cooking water to use in place of the liquid that canned chickpeas are packed in.

Chef's Tip: To cook dried mung beans and lentils, soak the mung beans for a few hours in cold water, then simmer gently in salted water for 20 minutes before adding lentils and cooking for 20 minutes more.

Whole-Wheat Ricotta Gnocchi with Vodka Sauce

Makes 6–8 servings

Gnocchi

1½ cups (375 mL)
ricotta cheese, drained

½ cup (125 mL) whole-wheat flour

3 egg yolks

½ tsp (2 mL) salt

½ tsp (2 mL) chopped Italian parsley

Vodka Sauce

2 Tbsp (30 mL) olive oil

1 small onion, finely chopped

2 cloves garlic, minced

1 small jalapeno pepper, finely diced

salt and pepper, to taste

3 cups (750 mL) heirloom tomatoes,
finely chopped

¼ cup (60 mL) vodka
(preferably Schramm vodka
from Pemberton Distillery)

12 leaves fresh basil, finely cut

The sharpness of the vodka complements the sweetness of the tomatoes in this fresh and filling dish.

Gnocchi

1. In a mixing bowl, combine all the ingredients. Add more flour as required (but not too much) to achieve a consistency that is stiff but still slightly sticky.

2. Liberally sprinkle flour on a large cutting board.

3. Using a spoon, scoop out small portions of dough and use another spoon to shape into quenelles (rugby ball shape). Place quenelles on the floured cutting board.

4. Boil a large pot of salted water and add gnocchi in batches. Don't crowd the pot or they may stick together or not cook properly.

5. Cook for about 7–8 minutes. To check if they're finished, cut them in half and make sure they don't have a gummy texture.

6. Remove with a slotted spoon and set aside on a large plate or tray.

Vodka Sauce

1. Heat a large pan and add olive oil followed by onion, garlic, and jalapeno, then season with salt and pepper. Cook for 3–5 minutes over medium heat, until onions are translucent.

2. Add tomatoes and cook for 10 minutes more, just until they are soft.

3. Add vodka and cook for an additional 5 minutes.

4. Stir in basil and adjust seasoning if required.

5. When you're ready to serve, drain the excess water from the gnocchi and then add to your heated sauce.

West Coast Panipuri

Makes 6–8 servings

East meets West in these delicious appies.

1. Brush all phyllo sheets with ghee and layer 3 sheets on top of each other, seasoning lightly with salt and pepper between the layers. Cut into 12 squares. Repeat process 3 more times with remaining phyllo sheets.

2. Place each square into a separate muffin cup and bake at 350°F (180°C), until golden brown.

3. In a pan, heat remaining ghee and add onion, ginger, and garlic. Cook until brown in colour and just beginning to stick to the bottom.

4. Stirring constantly, add curry powder, and cook for 3–4 minutes, then add coconut cream and bring to a boil. When mixture is boiling, add chickpeas.

5. In a large bowl, combine potatoes and cauliflower and pour coconut mixture overtop. Stir to combine, then add mint, coriander, and cilantro.

6. Spoon mixture into phyllo cups and garnish with additional fresh cilantro. Serve immediately.

12 sheets phyllo pastry

½ cup (125 mL) ghee or clarified butter

salt and pepper

1 small onion, finely chopped

2 Tbsp (30 mL) fresh ginger, minced

4 cloves garlic, minced

3 Tbsp (45 mL) curry powder

½ cup (125 mL) coconut cream

1 cup (250 mL) chickpeas

2 large potatoes, peeled, cooked, mashed, and kept warm

1 cup (250 mL) cauliflower, cooked and roughly chopped, warm

quarter bunch fresh mint, chopped

1 tsp (5 mL) ground coriander

quarter bunch fresh cilantro, chopped

Wendle House Coconut Bread

Miss Wendle, Barkerville

Makes 1 loaf

1 cup plus 2 Tbsp (280 mL) brown sugar, divided

1 cup (250 mL) butter

2 eggs

1 tsp (5 mL) vanilla extract

2 cups (500 mL) grated coconut, unsweetened

6 cups (1.5 L) flour

2 tsp (10 mL) baking powder

½ tsp (2 mL) salt

1 cup (250 mL) coconut milk

This is a traditional recipe from the 1800s. Coconuts were one of the only fruits that could survive the long journey to remote gold rush towns. To do as they did then, you'll need an axe to split your coconut in half!

1. In a large bowl, beat 1 cup (250 mL) brown sugar and butter until fluffy. Add eggs, vanilla extract, and grated coconut.

2. In a separate bowl, combine flour, baking powder, and salt. Fold half of the dry ingredients into the batter, then fold in coconut milk, followed by remaining dry ingredients.

3. Pour batter into a greased loaf pan and sprinkle top with 2 Tbsp (30 mL) brown sugar.

4. Bake at 350° (180°F) for 40–45 minutes.

5. Serve sliced with fresh berries and cream.

Julia Wendle was one of six siblings raised in northeastern Kansas by her widowed mother. Her brother Joseph left home in the 1890s and ended up in Barkerville. By 1906, he was well established as a miner and local entrepreneur. As an unmarried man, he needed a housekeeper so his spinster sister Julia made the trek to Barkerville to help him out—but just for this one mining season!

Miss Wendle gives Chef Steve lessons in baking, 1906 style!

Beer Scones with Blackberry Preserve

Makes 8 scones

Preserve

5 Tbsp (150 mL) sugar
2 cups (500 mL) blackberries

Scones

¼ cup (125 mL) Phillips IPA Beer
(or any other bold-flavoured beer)
1½ cups (375 mL) flour
1 Tbsp (15 mL) baking powder
½ tsp (15 mL) salt
5 Tbsp (150 mL) sugar
6 Tbsp (90 mL) butter, soft
1 egg, beaten
sugar, for dusting

Beer serves as a rugged addition to a somewhat lady-like dessert. The combination of your favourite brew and tangy fruit has something for everyone.

1. Prepare preserve by combining blackberries and sugar in a small saucepan. Moisten with a little splash of beer and bring to a rapid simmer. Do not stir berries, instead shake the pan gently so berries stay intact and as whole as possible. Cook blackberry preserve for approximately 25 minutes until thick and syrupy.

2. In a large bowl, or on a flat work surface, combine flour, baking powder, salt, and sugar, then work in the butter with your fingertips until the mixture resembles fine bread crumbs. Make a well in the centre and add the remaining beer, combining thoroughly, but without overmixing, to form a smooth dough.

3. Roll out to ¾-inch (15 mm) thick and cut out 8 shapes with a cookie cutter, or use a knife to cut into 8 squares or triangles.

4. Place scones on a parchment-lined baking sheet, brush with beaten egg, and dust with a little sugar before baking for 15–18 minutes in a 350°F (180°C) oven until well risen and golden brown.

5. To serve warm, slice open and fill with hot preserve, accompanied with good vanilla ice cream. Alternately, allow scones and preserve to cool completely and serve with clotted or whipped cream.

Tiramisu Cappuccinos

Makes 6 servings

Wake up your taste buds with a cup of coffee unlike any you've ever had before! Serve these impressive little desserts at the end of a dinner party.

1. In a medium saucepan, whisk together egg yolks, sugar, and vanilla until well blended.

2. Whisk in milk and cook over medium heat, stirring constantly until mixture thickens but *do not* allow to boil. Remove from heat and let cool.

3. Whisk mascarpone into cooled egg yolk mixture until smooth, and then add coffee.

4. Cut 12 slices of pound cake about ¾-inch (2 cm) thick. Using a round cookie cutter, cut discs that will sit flat in the bottom of a coffee cup or an individual serving dish.

5. Place 1 disc in the bottom of each coffee cup or serving dish and drizzle with Kahlua.

6. Spread half of mascarpone mixture over pound cake discs, and top each one with another pound cake disc and remaining mascarpone mixture.

7. Refrigerate for a minimum of 2 hours.

8. In a medium bowl, whisk cream until stiff peaks form.

9. In a separate clean bowl, whisk 2 egg whites until soft peaks form, and then gently fold into the whipped cream.

10. Spoon cream and egg white mixture generously over each "cappuccino." Sprinkle lightly with cocoa powder before serving.

3 egg yolks (reserve whites)

¼ cup (60 mL) white sugar

½ tsp (2 mL) vanilla extract

⅓ cup (80 mL) milk

½ lb (225 g) mascarpone cheese

2 Tbsp (30 mL) strong coffee, at room temperature

1 small loaf lemon pound cake (see Chef's Tip)

2 Tbsp (30 mL) Kahlua

⅔ cup (160 mL) whipping cream

2 egg whites

1 Tbsp (15 mL) cocoa powder

Chef's Tip: Any flavour of pound cake may be used in this recipe. Try poppy seed, or use ginger or orange paired with Grand Marnier instead of Kahlua.

Chewy Sunshine Oatmeal Cookies

Christine Hollmann, Terracentric Coastal Adventures, Lund

Makes 2–3 dozen large cookies

2 cups (500 mL) softened
(not melted) unsalted butter

2 cups (500 mL) organic
sugar or brown sugar

½ cup (125 mL) molasses

2 tsp (10 mL) vanilla

4 eggs

5 cups (1.25 L) flour

2 tsp (10 mL) salt

2 tsp (10 mL) baking soda

1 tsp (5 mL) cinnamon

6 cups (1.5 L) oats

1½ to 2 cups (375–500 mL) any
combination of the following:
toasted whole almonds (roughly
chopped), sesame seeds (lightly
toasted), sunflower seeds (lightly
toasted), unsweetened shredded
coconut, hemp seeds, dried cranberries
or apricots (finely chopped),
dark semi-sweet chocolate chips

An oft-requested recipe, these cookies are versatile in that they can be purely decadent with just the addition of almonds and chocolate chips, or you can add a variety of seeds for an energizing healthy snack for all your outdoor activities.

1. By hand or with a mixer, cream together butter and sugar, then add molasses, vanilla, and eggs until everything is well combined.

2. In a second bowl, mix together flour, salt, baking soda, and cinnamon, then combine with the butter mixture.

3. Stir in oats by hand, then add your choice of chocolate chips, nuts, fruit, or seeds.

4. Form dough into 1½-inch (4 cm) balls, place on a greased cookie sheet or parchment paper, and flatten slightly with the palm of your hand.

5. Bake for 10 minutes for a softer chewy cookie. If using coconut, watch the baking time as cookies will burn more easily.

Christine Hollmann is one of the owners of Terracentric Coastal Adventures in beautiful Lund, BC, at the top of the Sunshine Coast. The company offers a variety of recreational tours and educational and organizational development programs, all of which strive to foster connections between people in an outdoor environment. Providing tasty and healthy picnics for her program guests is a passion of Christine's, as is making real food from locally sourced, organically grown ingredients.

Coastal sunset in Gwaii Hanaas National Park Reserve

Pemberton Distillery Cocktails: French 75

Tyler Schramm and Lorien Chilton, Organic Craft Distillers, Pemberton

Makes 1 cocktail

1.5 oz (45 mL) Schramm Organic Gin

½ oz (15 mL) simple syrup (see Chef's Tip)

¾ oz (22.5 mL) lemon juice, freshly squeezed

Prosecco (or other dry sparkling wine), for topping the glass

lemon spiral (use zester or paring knife to slice a long, thin lemon spiral from a lemon)

Who better to make cocktail recipes than the people who make the liquor? Try both of these mouth-watering beverages with the Schramm products themselves if you can.

1. In a cocktail shaker filled with ice, combine gin, simple syrup, and lemon juice.

2. Shake well and strain into a chilled champagne flute. Top with Prosecco or sparkling wine. Garnish with a lemon spiral.

Chef's Tip: To make simple syrup, dissolve 1 part sugar in 1 part water. We prefer to use raw cane sugar. Steep chopped fresh ginger or rosemary in the simple syrup for a twist on this cocktail.

Tyler Schramm, owner and master distiller at Pemberton Distillery.

Pemberton Distillery Cocktails:
Schramm Spicy Caesar

Makes 4–5 cocktails

Clamato Juice

1. Combine all of the ingredients in a pitcher, stir well, and chill until ready to serve.

Caesar

1. Rim a highball glass with lemon juice and roll the glass in celery salt. Fill glass with ice and pour in vodka, then top up with homemade clamato juice.

2. Garnish as desired.

Pemberton Distillery is a boutique artisan distillery set in the heart of the spectacular Coast Mountains of British Columbia, specializing in high-quality, authentic, and distinct sipping spirits. Our philosophy is to source the finest locally grown organic ingredients and to create spirits that highlight the natural and unique character of the beautiful region from where they come. The distillery is family owned and operated and all spirits are handcrafted using traditional craft methods and hand-operated copper pot stills. "Field to glass" spirits include organic potato vodka (double gold medal winner at the World Spirits Awards), single batch organic gin, organic single malt whisky, and a selection of regionally inspired small-batch spirits and liqueurs.

Clamato Juice

3 cups (750 mL) tomato juice (canned or fresh)

2 cups (500 mL) clam juice

¼ cup (60 mL) freshly squeezed lemon juice

1 Tbsp (15 mL) Worcestershire sauce

1 Tbsp (15 mL) prepared horseradish

1 Tbsp (15 mL) barbecue sauce

1 tsp (5 mL) piri piri sauce (or your favourite hot sauce)

¼ tsp (1 mL) celery salt

freshly ground pepper, to taste

handful of finely chopped fresh cilantro (optional)

Caesar

lemon juice

celery salt

2 oz (30 mL) Schramm Organic Potato Vodka

6 oz (90 mL) homemade clamato juice

lemon wedge, pickled beans, stuffed olives, or caper berry, for garnishing

Resources

Interested in finding out more about some of the great places, chefs, and producers in this cookbook? Here are their websites to help you get started . . .

Barkerville, the living museum
www.barkerville.ca

Beaver Meadow Farms, Comox Valley
(home of Natural Pastures Cheese)
www.naturalpastures.com

Camosun College Culinary School, Victoria
camosun.ca/learn/programs/culina

Canadian Hazelnut, Agassiz
www.discoveryorganics.ca/growers/canadian-hazelnut

Carolyn Herriot, Zero-Mile Diet, Victoria
www.gardenwiseonline.ca/cherriot

Clair's B & B, Ladner
www.clairsinnladner.com

Country Grocer
www.countrygrocer.com

Covert Farms, Oliver
(a good source of purslane and peaches)
www.covertfarms.ca

Deerholme Farm, Cowichan Valley
www.deerholme.com

FortisBC
www.fortisbc.com

GFS Canada
www.gfscanada.com

John's Place, Victoria
www.johnsplace.ca

Kumsheen Resort (The Cutting Board Restaurant), Lytton
www.kumsheen.com

La Belle Auberge, Ladner
www.labelleauberge.ca

Local Lounge and Grille, Summerland
www.summerlandresorthotel.com

Locals Restaurant, Courtenay
www.localscomoxvalley.com

The London Chef, Victoria
thelondonchef.com

The Logpile Lodge, Smithers
www.logpilelodge.com

Manzanita Restaurant, Powell River
www.manzanita.ca

Mission Hill Family Estate, Kelowna
www.missionhillwinery.com

Nick Versteeg, Duncan
www.dvcuisine.com/dv-cuisine/bio-nick-versteeg

Old House Restaurant, Courtenay
www.oldhouserestaurant.ca

Pemberton Distillery, Pemberton
(makers of Schramm Vodka)
www.pembertondistillery.ca

Pentlatch Seafoods, Comox (Komo Gway Oysters)
komogway.com

Phillips Beer, Victoria
www.phillipsbeer.com

Quwutsu'un Centre, Duncan
www.quwutsun.ca

Rocky Mountaineer
www.rockymountaineer.com

Spinnakers Gastro Brewpub, Victoria
www.spinnakers.com

TerraCentric Coastal Adventures, Lund
www.terracentricadventures.com

Terrafina at Hester Creek, Oliver
www.hestercreek.com

Tourism BC
(you can access all the regions from within this site)
www.hellobc.com

Tria Culinary Studio, Comox Valley
www.triaculinarystudio.ca

Vancouver Island Salt Company, Cobble Hill
www.visaltco.com

Vij's Restaurant, Vancouver
www.vijs.ca

The Vinegar Works
www.valentinefarm.com

Watermark Beachfront Resort, Osoyoos
www.watermarkbeachresort.com

Woodwynn Farms, Victoria
woodwynnfarms.org

Yowza!culinary + concepts, Vancouver
yowzaculinary.com

Index

Acknowledgments

Cedarwood Productions would like to thank the following groups for their support of the television series *Flavours of the West Coast*. Without the TV series there would be no recipe book!

FortisBC has been a wonderful main sponsor. We've enjoyed learning about their sustainable energy developments and environmental initiatives. To learn more, please visit their website.

We would also like to thank Camosun College, Country Grocer, GFS, BC Ferries, and Liquor Plus for their valued sponsorship, and the BC Ministry of Tourism for their encouragement, knowledge, and advice on this beautiful province of ours. If you are inspired by our book to visit a new region of the province, do check out their website for ideas before you go.

CEDARWOOD PRODUCTIONS is an independent video production company based in Victoria, BC.

Cedarwood does all kinds of video work—corporate, training, and promotional—as well as television documentaries and the successful series *Flavours of the West Coast*, now in its third season. Cedarwood's heart is in creating programs and videos that make a difference, so it has been a great joy to create and produce *Flavours of the West Coast*, which highlights the wonderful work done by our province's food producers and chefs. We applaud the sustainable and local food trend and look forward to continuing our support by telling the stories of those who are doing it right. To learn more about Cedarwood, visit www.cedarwoodproductions.ca.